THE BREAKFASTS, DINNERS and DESSERTS WE LOVE AN

EVERYDAY CLASSICS

68 Tasty & Essential Recipes

GLUTEN-FREE, DAIRY-FREE, EGG-FREE and SOY-FREE

Written, Designed & Photographed by Alexa Croft
author of www.LexiesKitchen.com

kulia media
Printed in the USA

Published by Kulia Media, Fort Collins, Colorado
Inquiries & Wholesale Ordering: kuliamedia@gmail.com

ISBN 13: 978-0-615-90073-5

Printed and bound in the United States of America

Photographed and designed
by Alexa Croft, LEKS Creative
www.lekscreative.com

What are you hungry for?

CONTENTS

RECIPES AT A GLANCE

PAGE	EVERYDAY STAPLES	GLUTEN-FREE	DAIRY-FREE	EGG-FREE	CORN-FREE	SOY-FREE	TREE NUT-FREE*	COCONUT-FREE*	GRAIN-FREE	VEGAN
17	Seed Milks	👍	👍	👍	👍	👍	👍	👍	👍	👍
19	Nut Milks	👍	👍	👍	👍	👍	NO	NO	👍	👍
21	Coconut Milk Yogurt	👍	👍	👍	👍	👍	👍	NO	👍	NO
23	Whipped Coconut Cream	👍	👍	👍	👍	👍	E	NO	👍	👍
25	No Dairy Nacho Cheese	👍	👍	👍	👍	👍	NO	👍	👍	👍
27	Nutty Ricotta Cheese	👍	👍	👍	👍	👍	NO	👍	👍	👍
29	Condensed Cream of Celery Soup	👍	👍	👍	👍	👍	👍	👍	NO	👍
29	Condensed Cream of Mushroom Soup	👍	👍	👍	👍	👍	👍	👍	NO	👍
29	Condensed Cream of Chicken Soup	👍	👍	👍	👍	👍	👍	👍	NO	NO
31	Basic Gravy	👍	👍	👍	👍	👍	👍	👍	NO	E
33	Ranch Dressing	👍	👍	👍	👍	👍	👍	👍	NO	👍
33	Wedge Salad	👍	👍	👍	👍	👍	👍	👍	NO	E
35	No-Peanuts Butter	👍	👍	👍	👍	👍	NO	👍	👍	👍
37	Egg Replacers	👍	👍	👍	👍	👍	👍	👍	👍	👍
39	Gluten-Free Flour Blend	👍	👍	👍	👍	👍	👍	👍	NO	👍
41	Campfire Pancake Mix	👍	👍	👍	👍	👍	👍	👍	NO	E
43	Tortillas	👍	👍	👍	👍	👍	👍	👍	NO	👍
45	Loaf O' Bread	👍	👍	👍	👍	👍	👍	👍	NO	NO
47	Biscuits	👍	👍	👍	E	👍	👍	👍	NO	👍
49	Pizza Crust	👍	👍	👍	👍	👍	👍	👍	NO	👍
51	Pie Dough	👍	👍	👍	👍	👍	👍	👍	NO	👍

PAGE	BREAKFAST	GLUTEN-FREE	DAIRY-FREE	EGG-FREE	CORN-FREE	SOY-FREE	TREE NUT-FREE*	COCONUT-FREE*	GRAIN-FREE	VEGAN
55	Granola	👍	👍	👍	👍	👍	E	E	NO	E
57	Scones	👍	👍	👍	👍	👍	NO	👍	NO	👍
59	Chia Muesli	👍	👍	👍	👍	👍	E	👍	👍	👍
61	Oatmeal Cake	👍	👍	👍	👍	👍	E	E	NO	E

KEY: 👍 = **Safe** (when using certified allergen-free ingredients) E = **Easily Free** (with substitution) * SEE PAGE 6

PAGE	SWEET TREATS	GLUTEN-FREE	DAIRY-FREE	EGG-FREE	CORN-FREE	SOY-FREE	TREE NUT-FREE*	COCONUT-FREE*	GRAIN-FREE	VEGAN
113	Strawberry Cheesecake	👍	👍	👍	👍	👍	NO	NO	E	E
115	Banana Bread	👍	👍	👍	👍	👍	E	👍	NO	E
117	Macaroons	👍	👍	👍	👍	👍	👍	NO	👍	👍
119	Pumpkin Pie	👍	👍	👍	👍	👍	👍	NO	E	👍
121	Spritz & Sugar Cookies	👍	👍	👍	NO	👍	👍	👍	NO	👍
123	Mug Brownie	👍	👍	👍	👍	👍	E	NO	NO	👍
123	Mug Chocolate Chip Cookie	👍	👍	👍	👍	👍	👍	👍	NO	👍
125	Brownies	👍	👍	👍	👍	👍	👍	👍	NO	👍
127	Vanilla Pudding	👍	👍	👍	👍	👍	👍	NO	👍	NO
127	Chocolate Pudding	👍	👍	👍	👍	👍	👍	NO	👍	NO
129	Vanilla Ice Cream	👍	👍	👍	👍	👍	👍	NO	👍	E
131	Vanilla Cupcakes	👍	👍	👍	NO	👍	👍	👍	NO	👍
133	Graham Crackers	👍	👍	👍	👍	👍	👍	E	NO	E
135	Chocolate Cheesecake	👍	👍	👍	👍	👍	NO	NO	👍	👍
137	Marshmallows	👍	👍	👍	👍	👍	👍	👍	👍	NO
139	Flourless Chocolate Cake	👍	👍	👍	👍	👍	NO	NO	👍	E

KEY: 👍 = **Safe** (when using certified allergen-free ingredients)   E = **Easily Free** (with substitution)

A NOTE ABOUT THIS TABLE

This **Recipes at a Glance** table was created to help you quickly identify recipes suitable for your diet. Though great care has been taken to ensure the accuracy of the information provided, the author and publisher explicitly disclaim all responsibility for inaccuracies and oversights and ask that you verify the safety of all ingredients for your personal consumption. It is common for ingredients and manufacturer practices to change without warning, so please check ingredient statements carefully every time you shop. If you have questions about a product, contact the manufacturer.

*IS COCONUT A NUT?

By definition coconut is not a nut, but a drupaceous fruit. In my opinion it is unfortunate that the U.S. Food and Drug Administration (FDA) lumps coconut and tree nuts into one category—erroneously classifying coconut as a nut. Prevalence of allergies to coconut in the United States is low, and many with tree nut allergies can safely enjoy coconut. Therefore I distinguish recipes containing tree nuts versus coconut in the **Recipes at a Glance** table above. If there is any question about coconut reactivity, consult your doctor before enjoying a recipe in this book that contains coconut or a coconut by-product.

IN GRATITUDE

To those who inspired, encouraged and cheered me along in this endeavor, I thank you. To those who lifted me up with words of wisdom and hope when the journey got rough, you have my deepest gratitude.

To the **READERS** of my blog, thank you for your support. Your stories and feedback have brought tears of joy and gladness to my eyes. Keep up the good fight!

To **RECIPE TESTERS** Alicia, Amy, Andrea, Heather, Johnna, Joyce, Karibeth, Kimberlyn, Melissa, Paula, Sue, Tamara, and Tammy, you went above and beyond. Many thanks!

Thank you **ALISA** (my expert editor), **KIM, CAROL,** and my blogging comrades, I have learned so much from you.

Doctors **STEVE** and **MARY** Rondeau, we will forever be grateful we found you. To therapists and teacher **JANET, ERIN, LINDSEY,** and **LINDA,** thank you for the great help you have been to me and my son.

To **HANNAH,** a bright light in my life, thank you for your company in the kitchen. To **ANGIE,** my amazing friend, thank you for your love and support.

To my late father **CULLY,** thank you for passing the cooking gene on to me. I wish we had had more time.

To my **GRANDFATHERS,** I miss each one of you. I have kept your sage words of wisdom in my heart. To my **TUTUS,** thank you for instilling in me a love, first and foremost, for God and secondly for adventure and cooking. I hope I have made you proud.

To my sister **CASSIE,** one of the best cooks I know—I am in awe of you. To my sister **JILL,** thank you for being a faithful cheerleader and huge help in the kitchen. You are so generous with your time and love. To my brother **NICK,** dude, I am so impressed by you.

To **DAD,** thank you for inviting Mom and me into your life. Thank you for your love, guidance, silent strength and protection, and for being a loyal reader of my blog.

To **MOM,** my best friend and biggest fan. You are one of the most optimistic and cheerful people I know. Thank you for your support and for believing in me. I love you with all my heart.

To my **SOUS CHEF,** you bring me more joy than you will ever know. And to my **LITTLE MAN,** sweet boy, thank you for teaching me to "never give up." You keep your mamma laughing—and crying—tears of joy!

To my **HUSBAND,** you have been the perfect helpmate on this journey. You have taught me so much. Thank you for learning and growing with me.

INTRODUCTION

Stories of the pioneers who headed west in the 1800's captivate me. They were bands of brave souls, with nothing to turn back to and everything to gain by forging rivers, enduring the wind-swept prairies of Nebraska, and crossing the scrub lands of Wyoming, Idaho and Eastern Oregon.

On the bad days they held on to every ounce of hope in the good that lay ahead. They rooted their faith in the belief that one day the great Promised Land—Oregon's Willamette Valley—would unfurl before their eyes!

Perhaps you are embarking on a similar journey. It may have been a diagnosis of celiac disease, a sensitivity to dairy, autism, ADHD, IBS, or a slew of food allergies, that has led you to consider a change in diet. You are open to giving it a try, but perhaps fear obstacles that loom ahead—*half of the family just doesn't want to make the switch*, or *you simply cannot envision life without a certain food*. Feeling your plight and knowing how overwhelming it can be, I have written this book for you. With safe and tasty replacements for foods that brought you comfort in the past, and armed with recipes the entire family will enjoy, the more sure it will be that the dietary changes you make will stick. I don't want you falling off the wagon.

With challenges like the one you are faced with come some of the greatest blessings. It is rare to find a person who has been through a personal health crisis who did not change for the better. Had we never had to alter our Little Man's way of eating, we would still be feasting on Standard American Diet (SAD) fare. We would not be reading food labels, our freezer would be stocked with TV dinners, and we would still be getting sick multiple times a year. Little Man's health crisis was the best thing that could have happened to this family, and I can't help but presume that you will soon feel the very same way. As you set out on this transition, I hope you will keep my recipes in your back pocket (for many more, visit www.lexieskitchen.com) and these thoughts in mind.

HEAL YOUR WOUND

As an open wound to the foot would hinder your trek across the prairie, an abnormally permeable gut wall—or leaky gut—will hold you back from optimal health. Getting your gut into top shape is key. With an integrative doctor as your guide, lay out a map to recovery. It may include the adherence to a diet with a label such as Specific Carbohydrate Diet (SCD), Gut and Psychology Syndrome (GAPS) diet, Anti-Candida Diet (ACD), or perhaps one tailored to your specific ailment. It may include supplementing your diet with probiotics, digestive enzymes, vitamins, and minerals. With a guide, one tends to stay on course and the journey feels do-able and much less daunting.

DUMP IT AND MOVE ON

Back in the day, it was not uncommon to find dusty trails littered with fine china, chests of lace-trimmed dresses and burdens that proved utterly useless to the pioneering way of life. Similarly, the first time I purged our pantry I cringed at the food I was throwing out. Conveniences laden with artificial flavors, colors, and ingredients, including processed cheese and Oreos. Once you've made the decision to begin a new way of eating, a clean, pure, and safe pantry is the best place to start. Just dump the junk and move on.

DON'T GIVE UP

Healing the gut takes time. It may take months, even years. It took four years of ups and downs to get Little Man's gut in shape. Resist urges, with all your might, to leap off the wagon and return to the diet and lifestyle that got you where you were in the first place.

USE CHUCKWAGON STAPLES SPARINGLY

Though the chuckwagon carried staples such as coffee, flour and sugar, the bulk of a traveler's sustenance likely was bison, fresh fish, wild fowl, and foraged tubers and berries. In your journey to health, dip sparingly into the chuckwagon staples, and eat more fresh fare—organic as much as is possible—and if your diet allows, give yourself permission to enjoy a sweet treat once in a while.

COOK AROUND YOUR CAMPFIRE

Making the switch to cooking more meals at home will save your family money and give you greater control over what you and your family are eating. I try and make it a point to sit down to dinner as a family most nights of the week. It is a tradition our family has grown to love and take comfort in. It is a set time for each of us to share our day—the highs and lows—and to gather strength and courage for the morrow and the rest of the journey.

Little Man's Story

On a crisp September afternoon in 2006 a healthy, 10-pound, green-eyed boy entered this world. Early on we noticed differences in his development. At seven months his eyes began to drift (exotropia) and he grew floppy (hypotonia). There were delays in sitting, crawling, and walking. At 13 months he developed a case of "toddlers diarrhea" that lasted over two years (IBS). He acquired a stuffy nose and cough that would not go away (chronic sinusitis). He underwent MRIs and genetic testing. His immune system was on fire, reacting to nearly every environmental and food allergen on the skin prick panels. His little body had a difficult time regulating its temperature. He had no detectable reflexes in his lower extremities. He was often fatigued and developed asthma. His pediatrician said he would "outgrow it all" and that aside from speech, physical, and occupational therapy, we were doing all we could to help our son. Not comfortable with that counsel, my husband and I sought the help of an integrative doctor to explore the best of conventional biomedicine and alternative medicine. It was then that the journey to healing began. With a diet overhaul, supplementation, and targeted biomedical treatments, we began to see results! Today, Little Man's gastrointestinal tract is in top shape. He is absorbing nutrients, his hands no longer shake, and his balance is improving as is his speech. And with a healed gut he is able to tolerate many of the foods that once sickened him. It has been quite the journey and we are happy to report that a great valley is opening before us. For more of our story, visit www.LexiesKitchen.com.

INGREDIENTS & TOOLS

With a well-stocked pantry and the right tools you will be on your way to making magic in the kitchen. I encourage you to embrace the following ingredients and invest in a few tools that will help make the magic happen.

INGREDIENTS

Allergens are notorious for hiding in ready-made foods. The best bit of advice I received when we switched up our diet was to be vigilant in reading ingredients labels, and inquire directly with the manufacturer whenever cross-contamination was a concern. Additionally, if you are dealing with extreme allergies, beware of bulk food bins. Seemingly "safe" seeds, gluten-free flours, and gluten-free grains are often packaged alongside allergens such as soy, nuts, and gluten-containing foods. Most of the pantry items called for in this book may be found at your local natural foods store—all of them are available from www.amazon.com.

» Shopper Beware «

Here and in each recipe I bring your awareness to *possible* food allergens in certain ingredients with the ⊕ symbol. When purchasing these foods please double check ingredient labels and manufacturer warnings for cross-contact.

⊕ = SHOPPER BEWARE

AGAR-AGAR POWDER: A plant-based "gelatin" derived from seaweed. The powdered form is the easiest to work with and is the type I use in this book. It is often referred to simply as agar.

ALMOND FLOUR: Made from blanched, finely ground almonds, Honeyville (www.honeyville.com) offers the finest grind. Bob's Red Mill Almond Meal/Flour (www.bobsredmill.com) is also acceptable for the recipes in this book.

APPLE CIDER VINEGAR: Raw, organic and unpasteurized is best. Bragg Organic Raw Apple Cider Vinegar (www.bragg.com) is my favorite—it is full of raw enzymes and gut-friendly bacteria.

ARROWROOT STARCH: The easily digested starch of the arrowroot plant is used as a flour in gluten-free baking. It may also be used as a replacement for cornstarch in thickening sauces and puddings but, unlike cornstarch, should not be heated for more than a minute or its thickening power will begin to diminish.

BAKING POWDER: Hain Pure Foods Featherweight Baking Powder (www.hainpurefoods.com), with its potato starch base, is free of corn and aluminum.

BOB'S RED MILL ALL PURPOSE (AP) GLUTEN FREE (GF) FLOUR: The intent of this cookbook is to make your transition to a gluten-, dairy-, and egg-free diet relatively easy and hassle-free. A ready-made gluten-free flour blend is the ultimate convenience and Bob's Red Mill All Purpose Gluten Free Flour (www.bobsredmill.com) has proven to be one of the best performers when baking without eggs. It is a blend of garbanzo bean flour, potato starch, tapioca flour, sorghum flour, and fava bean flour. For the reason that it is produced in a facility that also processes tree nuts and soy, I have created a nearly identical homemade blend (see page 39) that you may make and use in its place.

BREAD CRUMBS: Hol-Grain Brown Rice Bread Crumbs (www.conradricemill.com) are what I use most.

BROTH: Examine labels as allergens are known to lurk in commercially prepared broths and bouillons. Pacific Foods (www.pacificfoods.com) is my go-to brand.

BUCKWHEAT GROATS: This hearty seed is a relative of rhubarb and contains no wheat or gluten. For the recipes in this book, use raw white buckwheat groats.

CANNED COCONUT MILK: My choice is Thai Kitchen (www.thaikitchen.com) full-fat coconut milk. It consistently separates—a must for yielding coconut cream (see page 23).

CHIA SEED: When ground and mixed with water, this nutrient-dense seed may be used as an egg replacer in baking (see page 37). Seeds come in black and white, with no significant nutritional difference between the two. I use white chia seed for baking because ground black chia seed can give lighter colored baked goods a pepper-flaked appearance.

CHOCOLATE: Enjoy Life Semi-Sweet Chocolate Mini Chips (www.enjoylifefoods.com) are free of the top eight food allergens. For cocoa powder, I buy Dutch process for its dark richness. If dealing with peanut or tree nut allergies, source cocoa powder from www.vermontnutfree.com.

COCOA BUTTER: This is the edible white vegetable fat of the cocoa bean. Ensure the butter you buy is food grade. Chips or wafers are the easiest form to work with.

COCONUT AMINOS: Can't do soy? Coconut Secret Raw Coconut Aminos (www.coconutsecret.com) are a pretty close substitution for soy sauce.

COCONUT BUTTER: This melt-in-your mouth spread is simply dried, ground coconut meat, not to be confused with coconut oil. Artisana (www.artisanafoods.com) is a good choice; however, it is processed alongside tree nuts. Learn how to make your own at www.lexieskitchen.com.

COCONUT FLOUR: Coconut meat is dried, defatted and then ground to create this dense flour. It is high in fiber and low in digestible carbohydrates.

EXTRACTS, FLAVORINGS & SPICES: Check labels to ensure these ingredients are allergen-free. Imitation almond extract is generally regarded as safe for those with tree nut allergies when made from the kernels of peaches and apricots. That said, some with severe nut allergies have claimed to react to imitation almond extract.

FLAXSEED: When mixed with water, ground flaxseed may be used in place of eggs in baked goods. The oils in flaxseed are fragile and go rancid quickly. For this reason grind flaxseed in a clean coffee or spice grinder as needed. If you must buy pre-ground flaxseed, store it in an airtight container in the freezer to ensure freshness. While flaxseed oil should never be heated, whole and ground flaxseed have been found to be fairly heat stable and suitable for use in baking without damaging the seed's alpha lipoic acid (ALA) content (Source: www.whfoods.org).

GARBANZO BEAN FLOUR: This protein-rich flour is made from dried chickpeas (garbanzo beans). Authentic Foods (www.authenticfoods.com) is an allergen-free supplier of garbanzo flour and many other gluten-free flours.

GRANULATED SUGAR: Too much sugar is not a good thing, which is why I limit treat-making to a couple times a month and choose my sugar wisely. For most recipes in this book that call for granulated sugar you may use coconut sugar. It is lower-glycemic, slightly less sweet than cane sugar and has a lovely caramel undertone. However, I specify cane sugar in some recipes where I feel it produces a more aesthetic result and classic taste.

GUAR GUM: This natural thickening agent derived from the seed of the guar bean offers eight times the thickening power of cornstarch and ups the "creamy" factor of dressings and nondairy ice creams.

HONEY: Buy raw. Buy local. If making treats for a child under one year of age, use pure maple syrup in place of honey. In the **Recipes at a Glance** table (page 4), recipes marked "E" in the Vegan column may easily be adapted to be vegan by substituting pure maple syrup for honey.

MAYONNAISE: There are a number of egg-free mayonnaise substitutes on the market. Soy-Free Vegenaise (www.followyourheart.com) is my preference and is carried by most natural foods stores in the refrigerated section.

NONDAIRY MILK: On pages 17 and 19 I explain how easy it is to make nut- and seed-based milks. Occasionally I opt for convenience and purchase ready-made. Unsweetened hemp, coconut, and almond milks are my favorite.

NONDAIRY YOGURT: I love homemade, additive-free Coconut Milk Yogurt (see page 21), but in a pinch will use SoDelicious Plain Cultured Coconut Milk (www.sodeliciousdairyfree.com) or Almond Dream Plain Non-Dairy Yogurt (www.tastethedream.com) in my recipes.

NUTS AND SEEDS: Nuts and seeds are best stored in an airtight container in the freezer. If cross-contact with gluten and other allergens is a concern for you, steer clear of bulk food bins. Gerbs (www.mygerbs.com) is a great source for seeds and runs an allergen-free production line. Nuts.com carries certified gluten-free nuts and seeds.

NUTRITIONAL YEAST: These yellow flakes of deactivated yeast impart a strong nutty, cheesy, and creamy flavor. I prefer Bragg Premium Nutritional Yeast (www.bragg.com).

OATS: Oats are inherently gluten-free, but can become contaminated with gluten when grown and processed alongside gluten-containing grains. Bob's Red Mill Gluten-Free Oats (www.bobsredmill.com) and GF Harvest (www.glutenfreeoats.com) are certified gluten-free.

OILS & FATS: Pick the right oil for the job. Pay particular attention to smoke point—the temperature at which a bluish smoke is produced and carcinogens form. This also marks the beginning of both flavor and nutritional degradation. Over time, most oils go rancid. To ensure freshness, buy smaller bottles of oil and store them in a cool, dark spot. As much as possible, buy from suppliers that support organic and sustainable farming. My go-to palm shortening is non-hydrogenated Spectrum Organic All Vegetable Shortening (www.spectrumorganics.com).

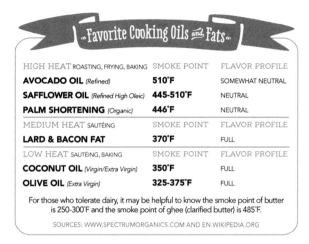

Favorite Cooking Oils and Fats

HIGH HEAT ROASTING, FRYING, BAKING	SMOKE POINT	FLAVOR PROFILE
AVOCADO OIL (Refined)	510°F	SOMEWHAT NEUTRAL
SAFFLOWER OIL (Refined High Oleic)	445-510°F	NEUTRAL
PALM SHORTENING (Organic)	446°F	NEUTRAL
MEDIUM HEAT SAUTÉING	SMOKE POINT	FLAVOR PROFILE
LARD & BACON FAT	370°F	FULL
LOW HEAT SAUTÉING, BAKING	SMOKE POINT	FLAVOR PROFILE
COCONUT OIL (Virgin/Extra Virgin)	350°F	FULL
OLIVE OIL (Extra Virgin)	325-375°F	FULL

For those who tolerate dairy, it may be helpful to know the smoke point of butter is 250-300°F and the smoke point of ghee (clarified butter) is 485°F.

SOURCES: WWW.SPECTRUMORGANICS.COM AND EN.WIKIPEDIA.ORG

PASTA: Tinkyada (www.tinkyada.com) brown rice pastas perform beautifully. If corn is tolerated, try the truRoots (www.truroots.com) line of ancient grain pastas.

POTATO STARCH: Potato starch should not be confused with potato flour. It is used as a thickener for sauces, soups, and stews and adds moistness to gluten-free baked goods.

WHOLE PSYLLIUM HUSK: Husks of the Plantago Ovata seed become mucilaginous when combined with liquid. In gluten- and egg-free baking, whole psyllium husk gives baked goods a chewier texture and fantastic structure.

QUINOA FLAKES: Quinoa is a gluten-free, edible, starchy seed native to South America. Similar to how quick oats are processed, quinoa grains are steam-rolled into quick-cooking flakes. Try Ancient Harvest Quinoa Flakes (www. quinoa.net).

RICE BRAN: The bran is the layer between the inner rice grain and the outer hull that packs over half of the nutrients found in each rice kernel. Because the unstable oils in rice bran quickly spoil, store in an airtight container in the freezer.

SEASONED COATING MIX: Try Hodgson Mill Gluten Free Seasoned Coating Mix (www.hodgsonmill.com).

SHREDDED COCONUT: Look for "finely shredded" and steer clear of anything that says "sweetened."

SORGHUM FLOUR: This very smooth, mild-tasting gluten-free flour performs like a champ in baked goods.

SUPERFINE BROWN RICE FLOUR: The key word here is "superfine." Authentic Foods Superfine Brown Rice Flour (www.authenticfoods.com) is the one flour I splurge on. It is worth every penny and produces grit-free baked goods.

SWEET RICE FLOUR: Though it is also called glutinous rice flour for its glue-like properties, it does not contain gluten. It is milled from a variety of rice that is especially sticky when cooked.

TAPIOCA FLOUR: Otherwise known as tapioca starch, this slightly sweet, starchy, white flour is extracted from the root of the cassava plant. Tapioca flour helps bind and improves the texture of gluten-free baked goods, and is smooth enough to beautifully thicken pie fillings.

TEFF (WHOLE GRAIN AND FLOUR): This ancient grain, and native to Ethiopia, is higher in protein than wheat and packs twice as much iron. At this time, brown whole grain teff and teff flour are most readily available in the U.S. and are what I use.

VANILLA POWDER: Authentic Foods Vanilla Powder (authenticfoods.com) tastes and smells heavenly! I use it in baking and add it to smoothies.

YOGURT STARTER: GI ProStart Yogurt Starter (www.giprohealth.com) delivers very consistent results. Though gluten-free, corn-free and soy-free, this starter is recognized to have exposure to some dairy peptones (broken down molecular structures) during fermentation. However, the final culture is filtered and contains less than detectable levels of dairy proteins. Per the manufacturer, yogurt made with GI ProStart is considered to be dairy-free based on industry standards. Some have success culturing non-dairy milk with probiotic supplements. I have found it to be hit or miss and prefer banking the success of my nondairy yogurt on a starter intended for yogurt making.

TOOLS

Every cook has their favorite tools and the right ones for the job can make all the difference. This rather eclectic list represents the kitchen gadgets I use and rely on the most.

HIGH-POWERED BLENDER: My Blendtec high-powered blender (www.blendtec.com)—comparable to a Vitamix—is my most coveted piece of kitchen equipment. It is a workhorse that produces super smooth sauces, soups, batters, and smoothies. It has been one of the best investments I have made in my kitchen and for my family's health. Many of the recipes in this book require one for optimal results. I look at it as a necessary tool for preparing many allergen-free substitutes.

BRAISER: An enamel coated cast iron Le Creuset 3½ quart braiser (www.lecreuset.com) goes from stovetop to oven, making it perfect for sautéing, roasting, and whipping up weeknight skillet meals. I use mine multiple times a day.

COFFEE GRINDER: I have a coffee grinder reserved exclusively for grinding chia seeds, flaxseeds, pumpkin seeds, sunflower seeds, and nuts to flours and meals. My $20 Krups (www.krups.com) model has served me well.

COOKIE DOUGH SCOOP: This handy gadget scoops more than cookie dough and batter. I especially like using a 1½ tablespoon scoop for making even-sized meatballs.

DIGITAL THERMOMETER: This is a must-have tool for temperature sensitive recipes. Invest in one that is waterproof.

ELECTRIC MIXER: When you have to beat it, an electric hand mixer or stand mixer is essential.

FOOD PROCESSOR: My Cuisinart (www.cuisinart.com) has been running strong for over 10 years. Opt for at least a 10-cup capacity machine.

ICE CREAM MAKER: I use a Cuisinart (www.cuisinart.com) 1½ quart ice cream maker. Look for a barely used machine at your local thrift shop, you just might get lucky.

METAL TURNER: A short handled, stainless steel turner or sturdy stainless steel cookie spatula is a great tool to have in your back pocket. It's great for flipping pancakes, turning meat, and scraping up crispy bits from a cast iron skillet.

NUT MILK BAG: I recommend the Amazing Nut-Milk Bag (www.purejoyplanet.com) or an extra fine mesh nylon bag for removing pulp and creating smooth nut and seed milks.

OVEN THERMOMETER: I've never met an oven with an interior temperature that was spot on.

EVERYDAY STAPLES

This collection of "foundation recipes" is the backbone of, or accompaniment to, many of the recipes found in this book. You will find gluten-free, dairy-free and egg-free substitutes for indispensable kitchen staples like yogurt, peanut butter, pie dough and sandwich bread.

Chocolate Milk

Add two tablespoons cocoa powder and sweetener of choice for a creamy and nutritious chocolate milk.

Seed Milks

Choice of raw **seeds** (see Tips and Tricks)

3-4 cups **water**

Pinch of **salt**

1 teaspoon **vanilla extract**, optional

Sweetener, optional (see page 18)

It has been encouraging to see seed milks such as hemp and sunflower go mainstream. I purchase a box on occasion to keep on hand for convenience, however making it requires very little effort and is 100% additive-free.

1. Soak, rinse, and drain seeds (see Tips and Tricks below for soaking times).

2. In the container of a high-powered blender combine seeds, 3 cups water, salt, vanilla extract, and sweetener to taste. Cover and blend on high 1-2 minutes or until super smooth.

3. Pour mixture through a nut milk bag (see page 14), into a large wide-mouth bowl. Gently squeeze to extract milk.

4. Thin with additional 1 cup water if desired.

5. Keeps up to 5 days in a tightly covered jar in refrigerator.

SOAKING TIMES FOR SEEDS

Hulled Sunflower > 1 cup > soak 6-8 hours

Hulled Pumpkin > 1 cup > soak 6-8 hours

Hulled Hemp > 3/4 cup > soak 6-8 hours

A Touch of Sweet

Blending in pitted dates, honey, maple syrup or liquid stevia are all great ways to add a hint of sweet to plant-based milks.

Nut Milks

Raw **nuts** (see Tips and Tricks)

3-4 cups **water**

Pinch **salt**

 1 teaspoon **vanilla extract**, optional

Sweetener, optional (see opposite page)

Hands down, nuts make the creamiest and richest plant-based milks. Cashew milk is a great one to start with as it does not require straining when made in a high-powered blender. At some point, do give fresh coconut milk a try. There's nothing like it!

1. Soak, rinse, and drain nuts (see Tips and Tricks for soaking times).
2. In the container of a high-powered blender combine nuts, 3 cups water, salt, vanilla extract, and sweetener to taste. Cover and blend on high 1-2 minutes or until super smooth.
3. Pour mixture through a nut milk bag (see page 14), into a large wide-mouth bowl. Gently squeeze to extract milk.
4. Thin with additional 1 cup water if desired.
5. Keeps up to 5 days in a tightly covered jar in refrigerator.

» Tips and Tricks «

SOAKING TIMES FOR NUTS

☞ *Almond, Cashew, Hazelnut and Pecan > 1 cup > soak 6-8 hours*

☞ *Macadamia > 1 cup > no soaking required*

☞ *Fresh Coconut Meat from 1 mature coconut > no soaking required*

☞ *Dried Coconut, shredded or flaked > 1 cup > no soaking required*

Look, Smell, Taste

As with any cultured food, yogurt should look, smell and taste clean. It should be slightly tart with no discoloration.

Coconut Milk Yogurt

MAKES: ABOUT 6½ CUPS | ACTIVE TIME: 15 MINUTES | TOTAL TIME: 14-20 HOURS

3 cups distilled **water**

3 tablespoons **tapioca flour**

1½ tablespoons **granulated sugar**

¾ teaspoon **agar powder**

2 (14 oz) cans full-fat **coconut milk**

⅛ heaping teaspoon **GI ProStart Yogurt Starter** (see page 14)

If you've gone dairy free and miss yogurt, give this recipe a try. With a culturing window of 8 to 10 hours, I like to get coconut yogurt into the yogurt maker early in the morning to culture most of the day; or late in the evening to culture overnight.

_____

1. Sterilize all utensils and container(s) by carefully dousing in boiling water.

2. In a 4-quart or larger saucepan whisk distilled water, tapioca flour, sugar, and agar. Whisking often, bring to a boil. Reduce heat and simmer 1-2 minutes.

3. Whisk in coconut milk and heat just until steam rises from surface.

4. Remove from heat and allow milk to cool to 95-100°F.

5. Sprinkle yogurt starter over surface of cooled milk and whisk thoroughly.

6. Pour into glass container(s), screw on lid(s), and place into powered-on yogurt maker. Leave undisturbed to culture 8-10 hours until desired tang is achieved. Do not exceed 10 hours.

7. Yogurt will be runny. Transfer to refrigerator and chill 5-7 hours. Yogurt will set and firm up as it cools.

8. Keeps up to 1 week in tightly covered jar(s) in refrigerator.

Whipped Coconut Cream

MAKES: ABOUT 2 CUPS | ACTIVE TIME: 10 MINUTES | TOTAL TIME: 1-2 HOURS

2 (14 oz) cans full-fat **coconut milk**, chilled

2 tablespoons pure **maple syrup**

1 tablespoon **vanilla extract**

⅛ teaspoon **almond extract**, optional

I exclusively use Thai Kitchen full-fat canned coconut milk for this recipe. Allow cans to rest for a day or two in a cool spot or for 12-24 hours in the refrigerator—taking care not to shake them. The "cream" should separate from the watery coconut milk and rise to the top. Invert cans and open upside down. Pour off the watery coconut milk and reserve it for use in a smoothie. The white solid that remains is coconut cream.

1. Following the tips above, scoop coconut cream out of cans into a chilled medium mixing bowl. Add remaining ingredients and beat with an electric mixer 3-4 minutes or until soft peaks form.

2. Chill 1-2 hours.

3. Dollop atop your favorite dessert.

4. Keeps up to 3 days in a tightly covered bowl in refrigerator.

" Tips and Tricks "

☞ *The addition of almond extract neutralizes some of the coconut flavor of the coconut cream. If allergic to almonds, consider using imitation almond extract which is most often derived from apricot and/or peach pits. Check with the manufacturer to be certain.*

No Dairy Nacho Cheese

1 cup raw **cashews**

¼ cup chopped **red bell pepper**

2 tablespoons **olive oil**

2 tablespoons **water**

1½ tablespoons fresh **lemon juice**

1 teaspoon **granulated onion**

½ teaspoon **salt**

¼ teaspoon **ground turmeric**

A high-powered blender is the key to a smooth, creamy, spreadable cheese. This vegan "cheese" may knock your socks off—it did ours the first time we made it! With it a world of possibilities opens up. Use it as a dip for veggies or chips, in place of the cream cheese filling in jalapeño poppers or dolloped atop nachos.

---

1. Soak cashews in a bowl of water for 2-4 hours. Rinse and drain.

2. In the container of a high-powered blender combine all ingredients.

3. Cover and blend on high 1-2 minutes or until super smooth.

4. Stop blender and use a rubber spatula to scrape down sides as needed.

5. Add additional water, one tablespoonful at a time, as needed to adjust consistency and aid in blending.

6. Keeps for up to 3 days in a tightly covered container in refrigerator.

Tasty Variation

Mix in ¼ cup diced caramelized onion or some of your favorite dip seasoning and serve with crudités or crackers.

Nutty Ricotta Cheese

MAKES: ABOUT 1½ CUPS | ACTIVE TIME: 5 MINUTES | TOTAL TIME: 5 MINUTES

1½ cups raw **macadamia nuts**
½ cup **water**
½ teaspoon **salt**
1 small clove **garlic**

Beware. What you are about to make and enjoy is sinfully rich and addictive! Serve with crackers or replace mozzarella with dollops of this "cheese" on your next Margherita pizza or dish of lasagna. This ricotta is made zippity quick as macadamia nuts do not require soaking.

1. In the container of a high-powered blender combine all ingredients.
2. Cover and blend on high 1-2 minutes or until super smooth.
3. Stop blender and use a rubber spatula to scrape down sides as needed.
4. Keeps up to 3 days in a tightly covered container in refrigerator.

Condensed Cream Soups

MAKES: ABOUT 2¼ CUPS | ACTIVE TIME: 15 MINUTES | TOTAL TIME: 20 MINUTES

FOR CREAM OF CELERY SOUP

2 cups chopped **celery**

¼ cup **water**

1¼ cups unsweetened **nondairy milk**

1 tablespoon **coconut aminos** *(a soy-free, gluten-free alternative to soy sauce, see Tips and Tricks below)*

⅛ teaspoon **dried dill**

FOR CREAM OF MUSHROOM SOUP

2 cups chopped crimini **mushrooms**

¼ cup **water**

1¼ cups unsweetened **nondairy milk**

1 tablespoon **coconut aminos** *(a soy-free, gluten-free alternative to soy sauce, see Tips and Tricks below)*

⅛ teaspoon **dried dill**

FOR CREAM OF CHICKEN SOUP

1¾ cups **chicken broth**

FOR THE ROUX

¼ cup **high heat cooking oil**

¼ cup **Bob's Red Mill AP GF Flour** or Gluten-Free Flour Blend (see page 39)

½ teaspoon **salt**

¼ teaspoon **ground white pepper**

When we changed our diet I hadn't the faintest idea how to go about replacing the Campbells variety of condensed cream soups in our family's favorite casserole dishes. Come to find out, it was easier than I thought.

1. *If preparing Cream of Chicken Soup, proceed directly to Step 3.*

2. In a medium saucepan over medium heat sweat celery or mushrooms in water until tender. Transfer to blender container along with milk, coconut aminos, and dill. Cover and blend on high until smooth.

3. For the roux, heat oil in saucepan over medium heat. Whisk in flour, salt, and pepper. Cook 1-2 minutes or until mixture begins to bubble and thicken.

4. Whisk in liquid *(blended mixture or broth)*. Simmer 2-3 minutes or until smooth and thick. Remove from heat.

5. Use immediately or store in a tightly covered container in refrigerator and use within 5 days.

Tips and Tricks

For this recipe, superfine brown rice flour and most all-purpose gluten-free flour mixes may be used in place of Bob's Red Mill All Purpose Gluten Free Flour.

For more about coconut aminos, see page 11. If soy is tolerated, gluten-free soy sauce may be used in place of coconut aminos.

Basic Gravy

MAKES: ABOUT 2½ CUPS | ACTIVE TIME: 10 MINUTES | TOTAL TIME: 10 MINUTES

¼ cup **high heat cooking oil**

¼ cup **Bob's Red Mill AP GF Flour** or Gluten-Free Flour Blend (see page 39)

½ teaspoon **granulated onion**

⅛ teaspoon **ground white pepper**

⅛ teaspoon **dried dill**

2 cups chicken, beef, or vegetable **broth**

Need a quick-to-prepare gravy to pair with mashed potatoes or pot roast? Then this recipe is for you. I keep allergen-free broth and bouillon in the pantry for when I am short on time and don't have meat drippings or bone broth on hand.

1. In a medium saucepan, heat oil over medium heat. Whisk in flour, granulated onion, pepper, and dill. Cook just until mixture begins to bubble and thicken.

2. Whisk in broth. Continue whisking 1-2 minutes until smooth and thick. Thickness of gravy may be adjusted by adding more broth.

3. Salt to taste, especially if using low-sodium broth.

4. Remove from heat and use immediately or store in a tightly covered container in refrigerator and use within 5 days.

☞ *For this recipe, superfine brown rice flour and most all-purpose gluten-free flour mixes may be used in place of Bob's Red Mill All Purpose Gluten Free Flour.*

Ranch Dressing & Wedge Salad

MAKES: ABOUT 1 CUP DRESSING & 4-6 SALAD SERVINGS | ACTIVE TIME: 5 MINUTES | TOTAL TIME: 10 MINUTES

FOR THE RANCH DRESSING

½ cup **Soy-Free Vegenaise mayonnaise**

½ cup unsweetened **nondairy milk**

2 tablespoons **olive oil**

1 tablespoon **apple cider vinegar**

1 teaspoon **granulated sugar**

1 teaspoon **dried parsley**

¾ teaspoon **salt**

½ teaspoon **dried basil**

¼ teaspoon **guar gum**, optional for thickening

¼ teaspoon **granulated dried lemon peel**

¼ teaspoon **granulated onion**

⅛ teaspoon **garlic powder**

Pinch **dried dill**

Pinch **ground black pepper**

FOR THE WEDGE SALAD

Ranch Dressing (see recipe above)

½ cup **balsamic vinegar**

2 tablespoons **honey**

¼ teaspoon **salt**

1 head **iceberg lettuce**

1 cup **cherry tomatoes**, quartered

⊕ 1 cup crispy **bacon bits**

½ cup thinly sliced **red onion**

I make my take on the popular Outback Steakhouse Classic Blue Cheese Wedge Salad with this dairy-free ranch dressing. Along with the sweet balsamic drizzle, it adds to the "wow" factor of this great make-ahead salad. I serve a bowl of blue cheese crumbles on the side for those in the family who tolerate dairy.

FOR THE RANCH DRESSING

1. Combine dressing ingredients in a glass jar and shake well.
2. Refrigerate dressing for at least 1 hour to allow flavors to marry.

FOR THE WEDGE SALAD

1. In a small saucepan combine vinegar, honey, and salt. Bring to a boil and reduce to a gentle simmer. Cook until mixture coats the back of a spoon. Remove from heat and set aside. Glaze will thicken as it cools.
2. Cut head of lettuce into 4-6 wedges and arrange on a platter.
3. Top each wedge with Ranch Dressing, a drizzle of the balsamic glaze, tomatoes, bacon bits, and red onion.

··· Tips *and* Tricks ···

☞ *Make this salad vegan by replacing honey with pure maple syrup and omitting the bacon bits.*

No-Peanuts Butter

1 cup raw **sunflower seeds**

4 cups unsweetened finely **shredded coconut**

1½ tablespoons **coconut oil**

2-3 tablespoons **granulated sugar**

¼ heaping teaspoon **salt**

Who would have thought that a combination of toasted sunflower seeds and shredded coconut would produce a very close substitute—in taste and texture—to that of peanut butter? For the creamiest spread, use a high-powered blender (see page 14).

1. In a large skillet toast sunflower seeds over medium heat, stirring constantly, until most of the seeds are golden in color. Transfer to the container of a high-powered blender. Toast coconut over medium-low heat 1-2 minutes or until it begins to turn golden in color. Remove from heat and set aside.

2. Blend sunflower seeds on low until a fine meal forms.

3. Add coconut oil and blend on high for 10 seconds, turning off blender to scrape sides with a rubber spatula as needed.

4. Add 1 cup of toasted coconut. Blend at medium speed for 20-30 seconds then increase to high speed for 10 seconds.

5. Repeat Step 4, adding 1 cup of coconut at a time.

6. *As the blender works its magic, you may notice a fine oil mist wafting from the blender container. This is not smoke. That said, if the blender shows any sign of struggle, turn the speed down a notch.*

7. Add sugar and salt and blend on high until super smooth.

8. Mixture will be hot and runny. Pour into a jar with a tight-fitting lid. Cool at room temperature until firmed up. This may take 8-24 hours depending on the temperature of your kitchen.

9. Store at room temperature up to a week or in refrigerator up to a month.

Egg Replacers

MAKES: REPLACEMENT FOR 1 EGG | ACTIVE TIME: 1 MINUTE | TOTAL TIME: 5 MINUTES

FOR ONE CHIA GEL EGG

1 tablespoon **chia seed meal**

3 tablespoons **water**

FOR ONE FLAX GEL EGG

1½ tablespoons **flaxseed meal**

3 tablespoons **water**

"Gel" egg replacers are the backbone of my gluten-free baked goods. Though I would not venture to make a soufflé or quiche using gel eggs, they do produce fantastic results in a number of yeasted bread, quick bread, cake, and cookie recipes. Generally, for baked goods calling for two eggs or less, you are safe substituting 1:1 with gel eggs. For more information about chia and flax and how to grind these seeds into meal, see page 11.

1. Whisk ingredients until smooth.
2. Set aside 3-5 minutes until thick and gelatinous.
3. Use as you would one egg in baking.

» Tips and Tricks «

☞ *For aesthetics I use white chia seed and golden flaxseed for baking. When ground, black chia seed can give lighter colored baked goods a pepper-flaked appearance.*

☞ *The oils in flaxseed are quite fragile and go rancid quickly once ground and exposed to air and light. For this reason I suggest purchasing and grinding whole flaxseed and chia seed to a meal in a clean coffee grinder, spice grinder or high-powered blender as needed. Store whole flaxseed in an airtight container in the refrigerator. Whole chia seed may be stored in a cool, dark spot for up to 2 years.*

Gluten-Free Flour Blend

for use in place of Bob's Red Mill All Purpose (AP) Gluten Free (GF) Flour

MAKES: VARIES | ACTIVE TIME: 10 MINUTES | TOTAL TIME: 10 MINUTES

4 parts **garbanzo flour**

2 parts **potato starch**

1 part **tapioca flour**

1 part **sorghum flour**

DIY flour blends are not for everyone. If you prefer the convenience of a gum-free, ready-made, gluten-free flour blend, give Bob's Red Mill All Purpose Gluten Free Flour a try. This higher protein, legume-based blend is one of the most versatile out there. It lends great structure to baked goods—especially when use of eggs is prohibited. On the other hand, if you prefer mixing your own blend, have difficulty sourcing Bob's Red Mill products, or are sensitive to possible cross-contamination with soy and/or tree nuts (see page 11), you may use this nearly identical flour blend, cup-for-cup, in place of Bob's Red Mill All Purpose Gluten Free Flour.

1. Combine all ingredients in a large airtight container or zip top bag.
2. Shake well to combine.
3. For optimal freshness keep refrigerated.

☞ *When recommending legume-based flour blends I always preface with "don't eat the dough raw!" Uncooked bean flours, like garbanzo flour, can taste rather icky. But trust the process. Once cooked, the bean taste neutralizes and only the most sensitive of palettes would ever detect it.*

Campfire Pancake Mix

FOR THE PANCAKE MIX

9 cups **Bob's Red Mill AP GF Flour** or Gluten-Free Flour Blend (see page 39)

1 cup **granulated sugar**

½ cup ground white **chia seed meal**

2 tablespoons **baking powder**

1 tablespoon **baking soda**

1 tablespoon **salt**

1 tablespoon **vanilla powder**, optional

TO PREPARE THE PANCAKES

1 cup warm **water**

2 tablespoons melted **palm shortening**

1½ teaspoons **apple cider vinegar**

1 tablespoon melted **honey**, optional for extra golden pancakes

1½ cups **Campfire Pancake Mix** (see recipe above)

This mix was designed with the busy mom in mind—no eggs or milk required! If you've missed pancakes on your gluten-free and egg-free diet, the ease of this recipe will make you one happy camper. With this pantry staple on hand, you can whip up an impressive stack of flap jacks in a matter of minutes.

FOR THE PANCAKE MIX

1. Combine ingredients in an extra-large airtight container. Shake well.

2. Store in refrigerator or freezer.

TO PREPARE THE PANCAKES

1. Oil and heat griddle to 375°F.

2. In a large mixing bowl whisk water, shortening, vinegar, honey, and pancake mix just until combined—do not overmix. Let stand 2-3 minutes to thicken.

3. Gently ladle batter by the ¼ cup full onto preheated griddle. Cook until bubbles appear on surface. Flip and cook 1-2 minutes longer.

Tips and Tricks

☞ *One 44-ounce bag of Bob's Red Mill AP GF Flour equals 9 cups.*

☞ *Vanilla powder (see page 14) adds great flavor to this mix. However, you may omit it and in place of it add 1 teaspoon gluten-free vanilla extract when preparing the batter.*

☞ *Any neutral tasting oil may be used in place of palm shortening.*

Tortillas

⅓ cup white **chia seed meal**

½ cup + 2 tablespoons **water**, divided

3 tablespoons **palm shortening**

¾ cup **Bob's Red Mill AP GF Flour** or Gluten-Free Flour Blend (see page 39)

⅓ cup **sweet rice flour**

¼ cup whole **psyllium husk**

¼ heaping teaspoon **salt**

¼ teaspoon **baking powder**

You will love the versatility of these tortillas. Roll them super thin and you've got a high-fiber, pliable tortilla to stuff with your favorite taco or sandwich fillings. Roll them thick and you've got a fabulous flat bread or personal pizza crust.

1. Preheat a seasoned cast iron griddle over medium heat. Cut two 9-inch square pieces of baking parchment paper.

2. In a medium bowl whisk chia seed meal with ½ cup water and set aside 2-3 minutes. Using an electric mixer beat in shortening until creamy.

3. Add the flours, psyllium husk, salt, and baking powder. Beat to combine (dough will be lumpy).

4. Add remaining 2 tablespoons water and beat 30 seconds.

5. Push dough together to form a ball. Divide and roll into 8 equal-sized balls.

6. Place a ball of dough between the two sheets of parchment. Using a rolling pin, roll dough out to 6 inches in diameter (the thinner the tortilla, the more pliable it will be). For flatbread roll to 4 inches in diameter.

7. Peel parchment paper off of one side of tortilla. Place that side down onto preheated griddle and gently peel the other piece of parchment away. *For perfectly round tortillas, trim edges using an inverted 6-inch bowl and a sharp knife before transferring to griddle (gather scraps to make additional tortillas).*

8. For tortillas; cook 15-20 seconds on each side (any longer and they will be too crisp to roll). For flatbread; cook 1-2 minutes on each side.

9. Transfer tortillas to a plate and cover with plastic wrap.

10. Best enjoyed warm and fresh.

Loaf O' Bread

MAKES: 1 LOAF | ACTIVE TIME: 30 MINUTES | TOTAL TIME: 2 HOURS 30 MINUTES

2 cups warm (110°F) **water**

2¼ teaspoons **active dry yeast**

¼ cup melted palm shortening or **safflower oil**

¼ cup **honey**

1 teaspoon **apple cider vinegar**

¼ cup golden **flaxseed meal**

¼ cup whole **psyllium husk**

1½ cups superfine **brown rice flour**

1½ cups **Bob's Red Mill AP GF Flour**

¼ cup **rice bran**

1½ teaspoons **salt**

½ teaspoon **baking soda**

Determined to include a bread recipe in this cookbook, I set out on the daunting task of developing one that was free of gluten and egg. With the help of flaxseed, psyllium husk and rice bran, this beautiful loaf was born. With a happy dance I give to you a basic Loaf O' Bread—great for sandwiches or enjoying warm out of the oven with a dollop of jam.

---

1. Oil one standard 9x5-inch glass loaf pan.

2. In a large bowl or bowl of a stand mixer dissolve yeast in warm water. Whisk in oil, honey, vinegar, flaxseed meal, and psyllium husk. Set aside to thicken, 5-8 minutes.

3. Add remaining ingredients and beat to combine using a hand held mixer or stand mixer fitted with the paddle attachment. Dough will be sticky.

4. Transfer dough to prepared pan. Shape into a loaf and smooth top with moistened fingertips.

5. Place in a shallow warm water bath in sink. Cover sink with a large dish towel. Let rise 45-60 minutes or until doubled in size.

6. Meanwhile, place 2 cups water in an ovenproof baking dish on oven's lower rack to provide moist steam during baking. Preheat oven to 375°F.

7. Place bread on middle rack, over water. Bake 60 minutes, covering loaf with a piece of aluminum foil the final 20-30 minutes to prevent over-browning of crust.

8. Let cool 5 minutes in pan then turn out onto wire rack to cool completely.

Biscuits

1 cup cold unsweetened **nondairy milk**

1 teaspoon fresh **lemon juice**

¾ cup **Bob's Red Mill AP GF Flour** or Gluten-Free Flour Blend (see page 39)

¾ cup superfine **brown rice flour** + more for dusting

¼ cup **tapioca flour**

3 tablespoons golden **flaxseed meal**

2 tablespoons whole **psyllium husk**

1 tablespoon **baking powder**

½ teaspoon **salt**

⅓ cup chilled **palm shortening**

1½ tablespoons melted **Earth Balance Soy-Free Buttery Spread**, optional for brushing on tops

Slathered in jam or covered in gravy, these biscuits aim to satisfy. As with any biscuit recipe, take care not to overmix and overhandle the dough. Treating it with a gentle touch will result in biscuits that are light and tender. For buttery biscuits, and if corn is tolerated, use a tidge less salt and replace half the shortening with Earth Balance Soy-Free Buttery Spread.

1. Preheat oven to 450°F.

2. Combine milk and lemon juice. Set aside 3-5 minutes.

3. In a large mixing bowl combine flours, flaxseed meal, psyllium husk, baking powder, and salt.

4. Using a pastry blender or your fingertips; blend the shortening into the flour mixture until shortening is no larger than the size of peas.

5. Make a well in the center of the dry mixture. Add milk and stir just until a sticky dough forms.

6. With flour-dusted hands, gently push dough together and pat into a 1-inch thick disk on a flour-dusted surface.

7. Cut into 2-inch biscuits using a floured biscuit cutter or alternatively, use a sharp flour-dusted knife to cut the dough into squares or triangles. Gather scraps and repeat, handling dough as little as possible.

8. Transfer to baking sheet, spacing 2-inches apart. If desired, brush tops with 1½ tablespoons melted buttery spread. Bake 10-12 minutes or until golden.

9. Serve warm with jam, honey or sausage gravy (see page 71)

Pizza Crust

3 tablespoons **palm shortening**, divided

¾ cup warm **water**

2 teaspoons **apple cider vinegar**

¾ cup **Bob's Red Mill AP GF Flour** or Gluten-Free Flour Blend (see page 39)

⅓ cup superfine **brown rice flour**

2 tablespoons golden **flaxseed meal**

2 teaspoons ground fennel seed or **Italian seasoning**, optional

🔄 1 teaspoon **baking powder**

¼ heaping teaspoon **salt**

Good yeast-free pizza crust recipes are hard to find. After many years of experimenting I created this favorite. "Simple" and "quick" are understatements when describing this crust. There is no kneading of dough, no rising, no rolling or tossing. Simply blend. Pour. Bake. Pizza has made a comeback in this house. I hope it does in yours, too!

1. Grease a 12-inch round oven-proof cast iron skillet with 1 tablespoon shortening. Place skillet in oven and preheat to 435°F. The skillet needs to be good and hot.

2. Just prior to removing preheated skillet from oven, prepare batter by combining the remaining 2 tablespoons shortening and remaining ingredients in the container of a blender. Cover and blend on high 15 seconds or just until combined.

3. Working quickly and carefully, remove the hot skillet from oven and pour batter onto skillet. *You want to hear it sizzle.* Using a spatula, gently and evenly spread batter to cover bottom of skillet.

4. Return to oven and bake 15 minutes at 435°F.

5. Remove from oven and top with your favorite sauce and pizza toppings.

6. Return to oven and bake another 8-10 minutes.

»Tips and Tricks«

☞ *I find a blender handy for making this batter, but in a pinch a bowl, a whisk, and a strong arm work just as well.*

Cream Pie

Cream pie is making a comeback! Pre-bake pie shell and fill with chocolate or vanilla pudding (see page 127).

Pie Dough

MAKES: TWO 9-INCH ROUND PIE CRUSTS | ACTIVE TIME: 30 MINUTES | TOTAL TIME: 2 HOURS 30 MINUTES

1 cup superfine **brown rice flour**

¼ cup + 2 tablespoons **sweet rice flour**

¼ cup + 2 tablespoons **tapioca flour** + more for dusting

¼ cup + 2 tablespoons **potato starch**

3 tablespoons white **chia seed meal**

3 tablespoons **granulated sugar**, (omit for savory crust)

1 tablespoon whole **psyllium husk**

½ teaspoon **salt**

✿ ½ teaspoon **baking powder**

1 cup very cold **palm shortening**

Approximately ¾ cup ice-cold **water**

It is in a wheat flour pie crust that gluten really shines. So when you don't have it to work with, and are avoiding gums like xanthan and guar, chia and psyllium come to the rescue. This dough benefits from chilling and resting for at least two hours, preferably overnight, before rolling out.

1. In the bowl of a food processor fitted with the "s" blade pulse flours, potato starch, chia seed meal, sugar, psyllium husk, salt, and baking powder until combined. Add shortening and pulse 6-8 times or until nickel-sized clumps begin to form.

2. Add ½ cup plus 2 tablespoons ice-cold water and pulse 8-10 times or until a dough begins to form. Add another 2 tablespoons water, only if needed, to achieve a dough that holds together but that is not sticky.

3. Remove dough from food processor and knead 2-3 times on a flour-dusted surface. Divide dough in half and shape into two 1-inch thick disks. Wrap disks individually in plastic wrap and refrigerate for at least two hours.

4. Remove dough from refrigerator 10 minutes prior to rolling. Place each disk between two flour-dusted layers of baking parchment paper. Roll dough to fit pie pan. Remove the top sheet of parchment and carefully transfer rolled dough to pie pan. Remove second sheet of parchment and work dough down into bottom and along sides of pan. If the dough breaks apart, simply push it back together. Use remaining dough for top of pie or freeze for future use.

5. Refrigerate or freeze pie shell until firm before filling and/or pre-baking. Brush excess flour off with a pastry brush.

6. For a pre-baked crust, bake in preheated 450°F oven 10-12 minutes.

BREAKFASTS

Eggs and toast, milk and cereal—the threesome of wheat, dairy and eggs have long been the building blocks of what we call breakfast. Take them away and many are left asking "*what do I eat now?*" Take heart, featured in this section is a handful of recipes that deliver the morning meals you know and love and can enjoy again.

Granola

2 cups gluten-free **rolled oats**

1½ cups raw **walnuts**, chopped

1½ cups raw **almonds**, chopped

1 cup **quinoa flakes**

½ cup **honey**

⅓ cup palm shortening or **coconut oil**

✤ 1 tablespoon **vanilla extract**

1 teaspoon **cinnamon**

¼ teaspoon **salt**

⅛ teaspoon **ground nutmeg**

1 cup unsweetened **shredded coconut**

1-2 cups chopped **dried fruit**, optional

Granola is unbelievably easy to make and freezes well. For a breakfast that is filling, serve this granola atop a bowl of nondairy yogurt (see page 21) and fresh fruit. For a nut-free granola, replace nuts with a combination of raw sunflower and pumpkin seeds. For a coconut-free granola, omit the shredded coconut and use palm shortening instead of coconut oil. A cup or two of dried fruit stirred in after baking takes this granola to a whole new level.

1. Preheat oven to 275°F.
2. In a large bowl combine oats, nuts, and quinoa flakes.
3. In a small saucepan combine honey, oil, vanilla extract, cinnamon, salt, and nutmeg. Gently heat until coconut oil and honey are melted.
4. Give the honey mixture a good whisk and pour over the oat mixture.
5. Stir to combine and spread evenly on a rimmed baking sheet.
6. Bake until lightly golden, about 30 minutes, stirring every 10 minutes to ensure even toasting.
7. Remove from oven and stir in shredded coconut and dried fruit.
8. Let cool completely on baking sheet.
9. Store in a tightly covered container. Keeps best in refrigerator or freezer.

Scones

MAKES: 12 | ACTIVE TIME: 15 MINUTES | TOTAL TIME: 35 MINUTES

DRY INGREDIENTS

2 cups **Bob's Red Mill AP GF Flour** or Gluten-Free Flour Blend (see page 39)

1 cup **almond flour**

½ cup **granulated sugar**

¼ cup golden **flaxseed meal**

2 tablespoons **baking powder**

¼ teaspoon **salt**

WET INGREDIENTS

¾ cup warm **nondairy milk**

¼ cup melted **palm shortening**

1 tablespoon fresh **lemon juice**

1 teaspoon **vanilla extract**

Make Saturday morning special—serve up scones and tea for breakfast! A big bowl of fresh berries and Whipped Coconut Cream (see page 23) make it an extra decadent affair.

1. Preheat oven to 400°F. Line a baking sheet with baking parchment paper.

2. In a large mixing bowl combine dry ingredients.

3. In a small mixing bowl combine wet ingredients.

4. Add wet ingredients to dry and stir just until combined. Do not overmix. Dough will be light and sticky.

5. With moistened hands, divide dough in half and form into two balls. Throw, literally, each ball of dough down onto cookie sheet to form two 2-inch thick disks.

6. Using a sharp, wet knife, score each disk into six pie-shaped wedges.

7. Bake 16-18 minutes. Remove from oven and cut along score marks to form 12 scones. Serve warm.

Mexican Chocolate

Give this Chia Muesli a
chocolate kick by adding
1½ tablespoons cocoa
powder to the mix.

Chia Muesli

SERVINGS: ABOUT 7 | ACTIVE TIME: 10 MINUTES TO MAKE MUESLI & 3 MINUTES TO PREPARE

1 cup finely chopped dates or **dried fruit**

¾ cup white or black **chia seed**

½ cup slivered **almonds**

¼ cup raw **buckwheat groats**

¼ cup **quinoa flakes**

2 tablespoons **granulated sugar**

1 vanilla bean split lengthwise or
1 teaspoon **vanilla powder**

1 teaspoon **cinnamon**

Pinch **salt**

For years, boxed cereal was a mainstay in our home. The first time I purged our pantry I counted 10 boxes! Now an occasional "treat," we have replaced those cereals with nut and seed blends like Chia Muesli. Make it nut-free by replacing the nuts with raw pumpkin and/or sunflower seeds. You may opt to leave out the sugar and sweeten to taste with stevia or honey once prepared.

_____

1. Combine all ingredients in an airtight container and give it a good shake. Store in refrigerator or in a cool dry place.

2. If using a vanilla bean, allow it to infuse the cereal with its flavor for a couple of days. Do not eat the vanilla bean pod.

3. To prepare muesli; mix 3 tablespoons muesli with ¼ cup hot water or nondairy milk. Let stand 3 minutes to thicken.

Oatmeal Cake

SERVES: 4-6 | ACTIVE TIME: 10 MINUTES | TOTAL TIME: 50 MINUTES

1⅓ cups warm **nondairy milk**

¼ cup melted honey or pure **maple syrup**

¼ cup melted palm shortening or **coconut oil**

½ teaspoon **ground cinnamon**

½ scant teaspoon **salt**

¼ teaspoon **ground cardamom**

⚙ 1 teaspoon **vanilla extract**

⚙ ¼ teaspoon **almond extract**, optional

2½ cups gluten-free **quick cooking oats**

⚙ 1½ teaspoons **baking powder**

Cake for breakfast? Yes, please. This fiber-rich Oatmeal Cake makes for an easy and festive first meal of the day—especially when topped with fresh fruit and Whipped Coconut Cream (see page 23). The mix-in options are endless. Whatever you love stirring into your bowl of oatmeal, you can mix into this cake.

---

1. Preheat oven to 325°F. Oil an 8x8-inch glass baking dish.
2. In a medium mixing bowl whisk milk, maple syrup, coconut oil, cinnamon, salt, cardamom, and extracts.
3. Add oats, baking powder, and desired mix-ins (see Tips & Tricks below).
4. Stir just until combined.
5. Spread mixture into prepared baking dish.
6. Bake 35-45 minutes or until center of cake is firm to touch.
7. Serve warm.

Tips and Tricks

☞ *Some of our favorite mix-ins include ½ cup chopped nuts, 1 cup chopped apple, or ½ cup dried apricots.*

Chocolate Pancakes

For a special IHOP-style chocolate pancake, reduce flour to 1½ cups and add ¼ cup cocoa powder and ¼ cup gluten-free quick oats. Prepare following blender directions under *Tips & Tricks*.

Saturday Pancakes

MAKES: 14 4-INCH PANCAKES | ACTIVE TIME: 15 MINUTES | TOTAL TIME: 25 MINUTES

1⅓ cups warm **water**

2 tablespoons white **chia seed meal**

¼ cup melted **honey**

3 tablespoons melted **palm shortening**

2 teaspoons **vanilla extract**

2 cups **Bob's Red Mill AP GF Flour**
or Gluten-Free Flour Blend (see page 39)

½ heaping teaspoon **salt**

¾ teaspoon **baking powder**

½ teaspoon **baking soda**

In the beginning, the modifications we made to our son's diet threw my husband for a loop. Weekends were his time to cook breakfast. It was a tradition he enjoyed, but remove gluten, eggs, and dairy and it became a serious challenge. So when I saw my husband flipping picture-perfect pancakes one Saturday morning, I nearly broke into tears. "Those have got to have egg in them," I exclaimed. Nope. They were gluten-, dairy- and egg-free AND delicious! That's when I knew I had married a genius.

---

1. Preheat oiled griddle to 350-375°F.
2. In a large mixing bowl whisk together water and chia seed meal. Set aside 2-3 minutes to thicken.
3. Whisk in honey, shortening, and vanilla extract.
4. Add flour and salt and whisk until smooth.
5. Add baking powder and baking soda. Whisk just until incorporated.
6. Using a ¼-cup measure gently scoop batter onto griddle to form 4-inch pancakes. Cook until bubbles appear and begin popping on surface.
7. Flip and cook 1-2 minutes more. Best enjoyed hot off the griddle.

·» Tips *and* Tricks «·

Batter may be prepared in a blender. Simply add all ingredients to blender container <u>except for</u> baking soda and baking powder. Blend until smooth. Add baking soda and baking powder and blend just until combined. Pour batter from blender container for perfectly round pancakes.

Hearty Pancakes

MAKES: ABOUT 16 4-INCH PANCAKES | ACTIVE TIME: 10 MINUTES | TOTAL TIME: 20 MINUTES

DRY INGREDIENTS

1¼ cups **teff flour**

¾ cup **tapioca flour**

¼ cup **rice bran**

¼ cup golden **flaxseed meal**

✤ 1½ teaspoons **baking powder**

½ teaspoon **salt**

½ teaspoon **baking soda**

WET INGREDIENTS

¼ cup melted **palm shortening**

¼ cup melted honey or pure **maple syrup**

✤ 2 teaspoons **vanilla extract**

1⅓ cups warm **water**

You will never guess that these tender, stick-to-your-ribs pancakes are egg-free. They feature teff flour—a remarkable ingredient to work with. Incorporate this ancient grain in your diet if you are looking to up your protein and iron intake.

1. Preheat oiled griddle to 375°F.
2. In a medium mixing bowl whisk dry ingredients.
3. Make a well in the dry ingredients and add wet ingredients in order listed. Whisk just until smooth, taking care not to overmix. Let batter rest 3-5 minutes to thicken. Batter should be light and airy.
4. Using a ¼-cup measure gently scoop batter onto griddle and spread to form 4-inch pancakes.
5. Cook 1-2 minutes on each side.

☞ *These pancakes freeze well. Reheat in a toaster or microwave oven.*

Soaked Grain Waffles

MAKES: ABOUT 5 7-INCH WAFFLES | ACTIVE TIME: 15 MINUTES | TOTAL TIME: 9 HOURS

THE NIGHT BEFORE

¼ cup + 2 tablespoons whole grain **millet**

¼ cup + 2 tablespoons raw **buckwheat groats**

¼ cup whole grain **teff**

1½ cups unsweetened **nondairy milk**

1 teaspoon **apple cider vinegar**

THE NEXT DAY

¼ cup + 2 tablespoons **rice bran**

3 tablespoons golden **flaxseed meal**

½ scant teaspoon **salt**

1 large ripe **banana**

3 tablespoons **palm shortening**

✦ 1½ teaspoons **vanilla extract**

✦ 2 teaspoons **baking powder**

¼ teaspoon **baking soda**

For centuries, cultures of the world have soaked grains to make them more digestible. Preparation of these crisp on the outside, tender on the inside waffles begins the night before—making breakfast the following morning quick and filling.

THE NIGHT BEFORE

1. Add millet, buckwheat groats, teff, milk, and vinegar to the container of a high-powered blender.

2. Cover and refrigerate overnight.

THE NEXT DAY

1. Oil and preheat waffle iron.

2. Add rice bran, flaxseed meal, salt, banana, shortening, and vanilla extract to soaked grains in blender container (**do not** add baking powder and baking soda at this time). Cover and blend on high 1-2 minutes or until super smooth.

3. Add baking powder and baking soda. Cover and blend on low 5 seconds or just until incorporated. Let batter rest 2-3 minutes.

4. Pour batter onto hot iron. Cook 4-5 minutes or to desired crispness.

5. Repeat, oiling iron between each waffle.

» Tips and Tricks «

☞ *Use leftover waffles in place of bread for a PB&J or turkey sandwich.*

☞ *For a sweeter waffle use sweetened nondairy milk.*

Buckwheat & Oat Waffles

MAKES: ABOUT 4 7-INCH WAFFLES | ACTIVE TIME: 15 MINUTES | TOTAL TIME: 35 MINUTES

1⅓ cups warm **water**

2 tablespoons **palm shortening**

2 tablespoons **honey**

2 teaspoons **vanilla extract**

1 teaspoon **apple cider vinegar**

1 cup gluten-free **rolled oats**

¾ cup superfine **brown rice flour**

¼ cup raw **buckwheat groats**

½ scant teaspoon **salt**

2 teaspoons **baking powder**

Served hot off the iron, these waffles are crispy on the outside and moist on the inside. I actually prefer them to the egg batter Belgian waffles I used to make. They are much more filling and sustaining. Like a hearty bowl of hot cereal, they stick to your ribs. And not to worry, buckwheat is of no relation to wheat. It is actually a fruit seed hailing from the rhubarb family and is one of the best sources of protein in the plant kingdom.

---

1. Oil and preheat waffle iron.

2. Add all ingredients, except for the baking powder, in order listed to the container of a high-powered blender. Cover and blend on high until smooth.

3. Add baking powder. Cover and blend on low for 5 seconds or just until incorporated. Let batter rest 1-2 minutes.

4. Pour batter onto hot iron. Cook 4-5 minutes or to desired crispness. Repeat, oiling iron between each waffle.

Biscuits & Gravy

SERVES: 4 | ACTIVE TIME: 1 HOUR | TOTAL TIME: 1 HOUR

1 batch **Biscuits** (see page 47)

✵ 12 ounces **breakfast sausage**

1 batch **Basic Gravy** (see page 31)

On a cold fall day there's nothing quite as comforting and warming as a plate of biscuits and gravy. If you prefer a little heat, choose a spicy breakfast sausage to pair with the gravy.

1. Prepare Biscuits (see page 47).
2. Brown sausage in a large skillet. Continue to brown until some bits are good and crisp. Transfer to a plate and set aside.
3. Prepare Basic Gravy (see page 31) in the same skillet used to brown the sausage, scraping up any bits for added flavor.
4. Stir the cooked sausage into the gravy.
5. Serve over warm biscuits.

Breakfast Sausage

FOR THE SAUSAGE SEASONING

2½ tablespoons **granulated onion**

2 teaspoons whole **fennel seed**

1 teaspoon **salt**

1 teaspoon **garlic powder**

½ heaping teaspoon **dried sage**

½ teaspoon **granulated sugar**

½ teaspoon **dried thyme**

½ teaspoon **black peppercorns**

¼ teaspoon **ground white pepper**

⅛ teaspoon **ground allspice**

Pinch **ground cayenne pepper**

FOR THE SAUSAGE

1½ pounds ground turkey, pork or **chicken**

Sausage Seasoning (see recipe above)

2½ tablespoons **high heat cooking oil**, divided

A sausage patty paired with a nutritious smoothie (see page 75) is one of Little Man's favorite ways to start the day. I like combining two meats when making this naturally gluten- and preservative-free sausage—pork and chicken being my favorite combo. I prepare the patties using the Freezer Method described under Tips and Tricks below. It is mess-free and ensures my freezer is stocked with a quick-to-fix morning protein.

1. In a clean coffee or spice grinder, grind Sausage Seasoning ingredients to a powder.

2. In a large mixing bowl combine meat, Sausage Seasoning, and 2 tablespoons oil.

3. Shape into patties or follow the Freezer Method below.

4. To prepare patties, heat ½ tablespoon oil in a frying pan. Brown fresh or frozen patties on each side until cooked through.

⏵ Tips and Tricks ⏴

☞ Freezer Method: *Line a baking sheet with baking parchment paper. Use a small dough scoop to make 2-3 tablespoon mounds placed 3 inches apart on baking sheet. Cover with another layer of parchment. Press mounds into ¼-inch patties. Create more mounds on top sheet of parchment. Cover with a third sheet of parchment and flatten. Transfer baking sheet to freezer. When frozen, peel back layers of parchment and place frozen patties in an airtight container and return to freezer.*

Breakfast Smoothies

SERVES: VARIES | ACTIVE TIME: 5 MINUTES | TOTAL TIME: 5 MINUTES

CHEERY CHERRY SMOOTHIE

2 cups **water**

1 cup **nondairy milk**

1 cup frozen pitted **cherries**

1 handful fresh **kale**, destemmed

2 tablespoons **chia seed**

2 tablespoons fresh **lemon juice**

✪ 1 teaspoon **vanilla extract**

Sweeten to taste with **sweetener** of choice

PUMPKIN PIE SMOOTHIE

2 cups **nondairy milk**

½ cup cooked **pumpkin**

¼ cup raw **walnuts**

1 **apple**, cored and quartered

✪ 3 tablespoons **apple butter**

1 tablespoon pure **maple syrup**

Pinch **salt**

LEMON-AID SMOOTHIE

1 cup **nondairy yogurt**

1 cup **water**

1 handful fresh **kale**, destemmed

1 **apple**, cored and quartered

½ **lemon**, peeled and seeded

Sweeten to taste with **sweetener** of choice

A produce-packed smoothie and a side of protein is a great way to start the day. In smoothies that call for nondairy yogurt, I use my homemade Coconut Milk Yogurt (page 21) or the lowest sugar nondairy yogurt I can find at my local natural foods store.

1. Place all ingredients for your smoothie of choice in the container of a high-powered blender.

2. Cover and blend on low, increasing speed and blending until smooth.

3. Add 1 cup of ice and blend again until smooth.

☞ Tips and Tricks ☞

☞ *Kale and Spinach Cubes: To ensure you are never without kale or spinach for a morning smoothie, try this method of freezing; steam leaves just until tender. Remove with a slotted spoon and plunge into a bowl of cold water. Drain and transfer to the container of a blender. Cover and purée, adding just enough water to aid in blending. Pour into ice cube trays and freeze. Once frozen, unmold and transfer to airtight storage and freeze.*

☞ *Lemon and Lime Cubes: Buy lemons and limes in bulk. Juice and freeze in ice cube trays. Once frozen, unmold and transfer to airtight storage and freeze. I use lemon and lime juice cubes daily—not just in smoothies, but in everyday cooking. So handy!*

LUNCH & DINNER

This collection of savory dishes is dear to my heart for the reason that it is a compilation of my family's favorites. The boys dance around the kitchen when I announce that Chicken Pot Pies are in the oven. After his last bite of Stroganoff, my husband reclines in satisfaction and sighs *"you can make that anytime!"* I am addicted to Loaded BBQ Potatoes.

Chicken Milanese

SERVES: FOUR | ACTIVE TIME: 15 MINUTES | TOTAL TIME: 30 MINUTES

½ cup superfine **brown rice flour**

¼ cup **tapioca flour**

½ teaspoon **baking soda**

2 **chicken breasts**

5-6 tablespoons **high heat cooking oil**, divided

1¼ teaspoons **salt**

⅛ teaspoon **white pepper**

¼ teaspoon **garlic powder**

⅓ cup **water**

Top a mound of gluten-free pasta and marinara sauce with these crispy, flavorful filets for a no-parm Chicken Parmesan, or use them to recreate your favorite fast food chicken sandwich at home. Chicken Milanese may be dressed up in countless ways.

1. In a small bowl combine flours and baking soda.

2. Slice each breast in half horizontally to create 4 filets. Pound each filet out to ¼-inch thick. Set aside.

3. In a large zip top bag combine 3 tablespoons oil, salt, pepper, and garlic powder.

4. Add chicken to bag and shake.

5. Add flour mixture to bag and shake.

6. Add water to bag and shake.

7. Fry chicken in remaining 2-3 tablespoons oil over medium heat until both sides are golden brown and crisp, and chicken is cooked through.

Slow Cooker Stew

FOR THE STEW SEASONING

1 cup superfine **brown rice flour**

2 tablespoons **salt**

2 tablespoons **granulated onion**

2 tablespoons **sweet paprika**

2 tablespoons dried **parsley flakes**

1 tablespoon **garlic powder**

1 tablespoon **celery seed**

2 teaspoons **dried oregano flakes**

2 teaspoons **ground black pepper**

1 teaspoon **dried rosemary**, crushed

1 teaspoon **dried thyme,** crushed

1 teaspoon **dried dill**

FOR THE STEW

2 pounds 1-inch cubed beef or **bison stew meat**

6 tablespoons **Stew Seasoning** (see recipe above)

2 tablespoons **high heat cooking oil**

5 cups **water**, divided

6 cups cubed **potatoes**

2 cups chopped or **baby carrots**

2 cups chopped **celery**

3 cups **beef broth**

Where we live the deer and the antelope play—and roam right along with the bison. I started making this stew using beef but switched to bison after learning that it is higher in iron and vitamin B-12 than beef, chicken and pork. Preferably, source grass-fed bison or beef that is not supplemented with or finished on grain.

FOR THE STEW SEASONING

1. Measure ingredients for Stew Seasoning into a large jar.

2. Cover and shake to combine. Seasoning keeps for up to 6 months.

3. This recipe makes enough Stew Seasoning for approximately 4 batches of stew.

FOR THE STEW

1. In a large bowl toss stew meat with 6 tablespoons Stew Seasoning.

2. Heat 1 tablespoon oil in a large skillet and brown half the meat on all sides. Transfer browned meat to slow cooker pot. Repeat with remaining meat.

3. Deglaze skillet with 1 cup water, scraping up any crispy bits. Add this liquid to the slow cooker pot along with the potatoes, carrots, celery, broth and remaining 4 cups water.

4. Cover and cook on high 4-6 hours or on low 6-8 hours, or until meat is tender.

5. Salt and pepper to taste.

Hamburgers & Meatballs

SERVES: 4-6 | ACTIVE TIME: 10 MINUTES | TOTAL TIME: 30 MINUTES

1 pound ground beef or **ground bison**

⊕ ¼ cup gluten-free **bread crumbs**

1 teaspoon **salt**

¼ teaspoon **granulated onion**

⅛ heaping teaspoon **white pepper**

⅛ teaspoon **garlic powder**

Some recipes are best committed to memory for preparation on the fly. A basic seasoned burger is one of them. Double, or even triple, this recipe and freeze patties or meatballs for a summer's evening cookout or a quick weeknight meal of spaghetti and meatballs.

1. Add meat to a medium mixing bowl.

2. Sprinkle remaining ingredients over meat and mix in.

3. FOR BURGERS: Divide meat into 6 equal-sized balls. Place each ball between two 6x6-inch pieces of baking parchment paper. Flatten to desired thickness using a flat-bottomed glass or bowl. Grill or pan fry until cooked through.

4. FOR MEATBALLS: Roll into 1½-inch balls. Pan fry or bake at 400°F for 20 minutes or until cooked through.

⟫ Tips and Tricks ⟪

☞ *Make and Freeze Hamburger Patties: Line a baking sheet with baking parchment paper. Divide meat into 6 equal-sized balls and space 3 inches apart on parchment. Cover with a second layer of parchment. Press into ¼- to ½-inch patties. Transfer baking sheet to freezer. Once frozen, peel back layers of parchment and place frozen patties in airtight storage and return to freezer.*

☞ *Make and Freeze Meatballs: Line a baking sheet with parchment paper. Form 1½-inch round meatballs, place on baking sheet and transfer to freezer. Once frozen, place meatballs in airtight storage and return to freezer.*

Wendy's-Style Chili

MAKES: ABOUT 1¼ CUPS SEASONING & 6 SERVINGS OF CHILI | ACTIVE TIME: 20 MINUTES | TOTAL TIME: 4-6 HOURS

FOR THE CHILI SEASONING

¼ cup mild **chili powder**

¼ cup superfine **brown rice flour**

2 tablespoons **garlic powder**

2 tablespoons **salt**

2 tablespoons **ground cumin**

1½ tablespoons **ground coriander**

1½ tablespoons **dried oregano**

1½ tablespoons **paprika**

1 tablespoon **cocoa powder**

2 teaspoons **instant coffee**

1 teaspoon **celery seed**

¼ teaspoon **ground cloves**

¼ teaspoon **ground allspice**

¼ teaspoon **ground cinnamon**

¼ teaspoon **cayenne pepper**, optional

FOR THE CHILI

2 pounds **ground beef**

4 large **tomatoes**, diced

2½ cups cooked pinto and/or **kidney beans**

1 small **onion**, minced

1 cup diced **celery**

½ cup diced green **bell pepper**

2 cups **water**

¼ cup **Chili Seasoning** (see above)

This not too thick, not too spicy chili was inspired by the version found at Wendy's—a classic American fast food restaurant. Ground bison, turkey or chicken make excellent substitutions for the ground beef. Don't care for beans? Leave them out and add more meat.

FOR THE CHILI SEASONING

1. Measure ingredients for Chili Seasoning into a jar.

2. Cover and shake to combine. Seasoning keeps for up to 6 months.

3. This recipe makes enough Chili Seasoning for approximately 5 batches of Chili.

FOR THE CHILI

1. Brown beef in a large skillet. Add meat to slow cooker pot along with remaining Chili ingredients—noting to use only ¼ cup (or to taste) of the Chili Seasoning.

2. Cover and cook on high 3-4 hours or on low 4-6 hours.

3. Salt and pepper to taste prior to serving.

Tips and Tricks

☞ If kids will be enjoying this chili, consider using a mild chili powder. For a spicier chili, up the heat with more cayenne pepper.

Chicken Pot Pie

SERVES: 4 INDIVIDUAL SERVINGS | ACTIVE TIME: 30 MINUTES | TOTAL TIME: 45 MINUTES

One half recipe **Pie Dough** (see page 51 and be sure to omit sugar)

¼ cup **high heat cooking oil**

¼ cup superfine **brown rice flour**

½ teaspoon **salt**

½ teaspoon **granulated onion**

⅛ teaspoon **dried dill**

⅛ teaspoon **white pepper**

⅛ teaspoon **poultry seasoning**

3 cups **chicken broth**

2 cups cooked and chopped turkey or **chicken**

2 cups frozen **peas and carrots blend**

2 tablespoons minced **parsley**

This meal comes together in a snap with leftover turkey or a gluten-free rotisserie chicken, Pie Dough (see page 51), and frozen veggies. Kids feel mighty special eating these out of individual pots with their initials carved into the crust, however an 8x8-inch baking dish works just as well. On nights when I am feeling lazy, I omit the crust and just serve the cooked filling over steamed rice.

1. Prepare Pie Dough (see page 51) at least three hours in advance.

2. Preheat oven to 450°F.

3. Heat oil in a large saucepan over medium heat. Whisk in flour, salt, granulated onion, dill, pepper, and poultry seasoning.

4. Cook 1-2 minutes or until mixture begins to bubble and thicken.

5. Whisk in broth. Cook 1-2 minutes or until smooth and thickened.

6. Stir in chicken, frozen vegetables, and parsley. Heat through. Adjust salt if needed.

7. Divide mixture evenly among four individual baking dishes or ramekins.

8. Place pie dough between two layers of flour-dusted baking parchment paper. Roll dough to ¼-inch thick. Remove top layer of parchment and cut into four uniform squares.

9. Drape squares over tops of baking dishes. Cut slits in crust to allow steam to escape. Make decorative toppings with any leftover pie dough if desired.

10. Bake 12-15 minutes or until crust is golden brown.

White Clam Sauce

SERVES: 4 | ACTIVE TIME: 15 MINUTES | TOTAL TIME: 30 MINUTES

3 (12 oz) cans chopped **clams**

1 (6 oz) jar marinated **artichoke hearts**, chopped

3 tablespoons **olive oil**

1 large **onion**, roughly chopped

6 cloves **garlic**, smashed

1 tablespoon dried **Italian seasoning**

3 tablespoons fresh **lemon juice**

½ teaspoon **salt**

Ground **black pepper** to taste

Looking for a seriously easy and seriously good pasta topper? Look no further. Back in high school my best friend, Amy, introduced me to white clam sauce. I remember being impressed by how simple and flavorful the dish was. This is a spin-off of her Grandma Mancini's recipe, with marinated artichoke hearts and a splash of lemon juice added for brightness. Serve over your favorite gluten-free pasta.

1. Drain and reserve liquids from clams and artichokes.

2. In a large skillet or medium saucepan, sauté onion and garlic in oil over medium-low heat until soft. Add Italian seasoning and sauté an additional minute.

3. Transfer onion mixture to blender container along with reserved clam and artichoke liquids, lemon juice, salt, and pepper. Purée.

4. Return purée to skillet; bring to boil and gently simmer 5-10 minutes.

5. Add clams and chopped artichokes, heat through and serve.

» Tips *and* Tricks «

☞ *Suggested garnishes; red pepper flakes, garlic pepper, and minced parsley.*

Macadamia Cream Sauce

MAKES: 2 CUPS | ACTIVE TIME: 15 MINUTES | TOTAL TIME: 15 MINUTES

3 tablespoons light olive or **avocado oil**, divided

¼ cup chopped **onion**

1 clove **garlic**, smashed

1 cup hot **water**

1 cup raw **macadamia nuts**

2 tablespoons raw **white sesame seeds**

1½ tablespoons **nutritional yeast**

1 tablespoon fresh **lemon juice**

1 teaspoon **salt**

⅛ teaspoon **white pepper**

This silky alfredo-like sauce is rich and decadent and pairs well with poached and flaked salmon. This recipe makes enough sauce to top about one pound of pasta.

1. In a large skillet sauté onion and garlic in 1 tablespoon oil over medium-low heat until soft.
2. Transfer onion and garlic to the container of high-powered blender along with water, macadamia nuts, sesame seeds, nutritional yeast, lemon juice, salt, and pepper.
3. Cover and blend on high until super smooth.
4. With blender running at medium speed, drizzle in remaining 2 tablespoons oil. Increase speed to high and blend an additional 30 seconds.

Loaded BBQ Potatoes

SERVES: 4 | ACTIVE TIME: 30 MINUTES | TOTAL TIME: 1 HOUR 30 MINUTES

FOR THE BAKED POTATOES

4 large **Russet potatoes**
1 tablespoon **palm shortening**
Coarse **salt**

FOR THE BBQ CHICKEN

1½ pounds boneless, skinless **chicken thighs**
1 tablespoon **high heat cooking oil**
¼ cup **granulated sugar**
1 teaspoon **granulated onion**
½ heaping teaspoon **salt**
½ teaspoon **garlic powder**
⅛ teaspoon **white pepper**
⅛ teaspoon **allspice**
½ cup **water**
2 tablespoons **apple cider vinegar**
2 tablespoons **tomato paste**
2 tablespoons **molasses**
◑ 1 tablespoon **Dijon mustard**
◑ ½ teaspoon **hot sauce**

FOR THE CABBAGE SLAW

¼ cup **Soy-Free Vegenaise mayonnaise**
1 tablespoon melted **honey**
1 tablespoon fresh **lemon juice**
3 cups shredded purple **cabbage**
◑ ½ cup diced **dill pickle**

This meal in a bowl hits the spot every time. The chicken cooks simultaneously with the potatoes and the slaw takes all of 10 minutes to throw together. I often double the BBQ chicken portion of the recipe and freeze half of it for when I need to pull a meal together fast.

1. Preheat oven to 400°F.

2. Scrub, dry, prick, and rub potatoes with shortening. Season with salt and bake 1 hour or until fork tender.

3. Sear chicken in an ovenproof, covered braiser or dutch oven in oil over medium-high heat.

4. In a medium bowl whisk sugar, granulated onion, salt, garlic powder, pepper, allspice, water, vinegar, tomato paste, molasses, mustard, and hot sauce. Pour mixture over seared chicken and stir to coat.

5. Cover, leaving lid ever so slightly ajar, and bake 35-45 minutes or until meat is tender and sauce has thickened.

6. Remove from oven and shred chicken using two forks. Stir to coat evenly with sauce. For a thicker sauce return to oven, uncovered, and cook an additional 5-8 minutes.

7. In a large bowl whisk mayonnaise, honey, and lemon juice. Add cabbage and pickle and toss to combine.

8. Slice potatoes open and top with one scoop each of slaw and chicken.

Chili Mac Skillet

SERVES: 4 | ACTIVE TIME: 10 MINUTES | TOTAL TIME: 25 MINUTES

1 pound ground beef or **ground bison**

1 medium **tomato**, halved

¼ cup (1¼ ozs) raw **macadamia nuts**

1 tablespoon **tapioca flour**

1 tablespoon **chili powder**

2 teaspoons **sweet paprika**

1¼ teaspoons **salt**

1 teaspoon **garlic powder**

¼ teaspoon **granulated onion**

¼ teaspoon **granulated sugar**

⅛ teaspoon ground **white pepper**

2 cups **water**

⊕ 1½ teaspoons **hot sauce**

½ teaspoon **apple cider vinegar**

2 cups gluten-free **spiral pasta**

At one time, our pantry was stocked with Betty Crocker's Chili Macaroni Hamburger Helper. Today we make it gluten-free—and from scratch. I highly recommend Tinkyada Brown Rice Spiral Pasta (see page 13) for this recipe. It holds up so well. Just take care not to overcook it.

1. Brown meat in a large covered skillet.
2. In the container of a high-powered blender combine remaining ingredients, except for pasta, and blend until super smooth.
3. Add blended mixture and uncooked pasta to meat. Stir to combine.
4. Bring to boil, reduce to low simmer and cover. Cook just until pasta is al dente, about 10-12 minutes for Tinkyada Brown Rice Spiral Pasta.

Quick Prep Tip

Pick up a gluten-free
rotisserie chicken and shave
off a bit of prep time.
The average 4-pound
chicken yields about
3 cups of meat.

Chicken & Rice Casserole

SERVES: 4-6 | ACTIVE TIME: 30 MINUTES | TOTAL TIME: 1 HOUR 30 MINUTES

1½ cups uncooked white or brown **rice**

1 teaspoon **high heat cooking oil**

½ cup diced **onion**

½ cup diced **celery**

½ cup sliced **mushrooms**

2-3 cups cooked and chopped **chicken**

¼ cup **water**

1 batch **Cream of Mushroom Soup** (see page 29)

This is classic comfort food, and one of my go-to dishes for cold, winter nights or potlucks. No one will ever know that it's dairy-free. You may want to double the recipe as I am certain you'll have requests for seconds!

1. Prepare rice according to package directions.

2. Preheat oven to 350°F. Grease a 12x7½x2-inch baking dish.

3. In a large skillet sauté onion, celery, and mushrooms in oil over medium heat until tender.

4. Remove from heat. Stir in cooked rice, cooked chicken, water, and soup.

5. Spoon into baking dish and bake uncovered 25-30 minutes. Finish under broiler 2-3 minutes.

Teriyaki BBQ

SERVES: 4-6 | ACTIVE TIME: 15 MINUTES | TOTAL TIME: 45 MINUTES-5 HOURS

½ cup **coconut aminos** *(a soy-free, gluten-free alternative to soy sauce, see Tips and Tricks below)*

2 tablespoons melted **honey**

1½ tablespoons **minced ginger root**

¼ teaspoon **salt**

½ teaspoon **sesame oil**, optional

2-3 pounds beef, fish, boneless chicken breasts or boneless **chicken thighs**

Teriyaki marinade is so easy to make, and for a fraction of the cost when compared to the bottled stuff. Use it on chicken, beef or fish and serve with hot steamed rice.

1. Add coconut aminos, honey, ginger, salt, and sesame oil to a large bowl with a tight-fitting lid or to a large zip top bag. Stir or shake to combine.

2. Add meat to marinade. For fish, marinate in refrigerator for 30-60 minutes. For all other meats, marinate for 4-5 hours.

3. Preheat and prepare grill.

4. Remove marinating meat from refrigerator and discard used marinade.

5. Grill until cooked through, flipping once.

·· Tips and Tricks ··

☞ *If soy is tolerated and you prefer using a gluten-free soy sauce in place of the coconut aminos, omit the ¼ teaspoon salt.*

☞ *For a tasty dipping sauce, make a double batch of marinade. Use half to marinate the meat. In a small saucepan, bring the remaining marinade to a gentle boil and whisk in a slurry of ¼ cup water and 1½ teaspoons arrowroot starch. Return to a rapid boil for 15 seconds and remove from heat.*

☞ *When using chicken breasts or beef I like to pound out the meat prior to grilling. One of my favorite tricks is to place the meat, in batches, into an empty cereal bag or large zip top bag. Partially seal/ fold the edge of the bag under to contain the meat. Pound out with a mallet or heavy bottomed saucepan to ¼- to ½-inch thick.*

Tasty Skillet Suppers

SERVES: 4 | ACTIVE TIME: 10 MINUTES | TOTAL TIME: 30 MINUTES

BACON & KALE SKILLET

2 cups uncooked gluten-free **penne pasta**

◍ 8-12 ounces **bacon**, diced

2 cups destemmed and chopped curly **kale**

2 tablespoons **water**

¼ cup raw **sunflower seeds**

SAUSAGE & OLIVE SKILLET

2 cups uncooked gluten-free **penne pasta**

1 tablespoon **high heat cooking oil**, divided

◍ 12 ounces pre-cooked **sausage**, diced

¾ cup **black olives**, halved

¼ cup julienned **sun-dried tomatoes**

2 tablespoons minced fresh **parsley**

2 tablespoons **olive oil**

Salt and pepper to taste

Mmmm. Two of my favorite skillet suppers. For these one-dish wonders I reach for Tinkyada Brown Rice Penne pasta, it is one of the few gluten-free pastas that doesn't turn to mush when cooked according to package directions. Applegate Roasted Red Pepper Sausage really makes the *Sausage & Olive Skillet* shine.

FOR THE BACON & KALE SKILLET

1. Cook pasta al dente in salted water according to package directions. Drain and rinse under cold water.

2. Meanwhile, in a large skillet cook bacon until crisp. Transfer bacon bits to paper towel-lined plate. Reserve ¼ cup rendered bacon fat.

3. Add kale to skillet along with water. Sauté 1-2 minutes. Add bacon, pasta, and sunflower seeds.

4. Drizzle with 3-4 tablespoons of reserved bacon fat. Toss to combine and heat through.

FOR THE SAUSAGE & OLIVE SKILLET

1. Cook pasta al dente in salted water according to package directions. Drain and rinse under cold water.

2. In a large skillet brown sausage in high heat cooking oil. Add pasta, olives, sun-dried tomatoes, and parsley. Drizzle with olive oil. Toss to combine and heat through.

3. Season to taste with salt and pepper.

Zuppa di Italiano

SERVES: 6 | ACTIVE TIME: 20 MINUTES | TOTAL TIME: 40 MINUTES

1 tablespoon **high heat cooking oil**

1 large **onion**, chopped

2 cups **zucchini**, peeled and chopped

3 cloves **garlic**, smashed

4 cups **chicken broth**, divided

1 pound mild ground **Italian sausage**

1 cup **water**

1½ cups cooked **cannellini beans**

2 medium Russet **potatoes**, thinly sliced

2 cups destemmed and chopped curly **kale**

Salt and pepper to taste

The little noses in our family turn up at chunks of onion and zucchini. Puréeing vegetables and adding them to soups is a sure-fire way to get my kids to eat them. The puréed zucchini and onion in this recipe ads a subtle creaminess to the soup that I find reminiscent of Olive Garden's Zuppa Toscana. Use a spicy Italian sausage if you like heat. For the kids, we stick with mild. This soup pairs well with the Outback Steakhouse-style Wedge Salad on page 33.

---

1. In a large pot, sauté onion, zucchini, and garlic in oil until tender. Transfer to blender container along with 2 cups chicken broth. Cover and purée.

2. Add sausage to pot and brown until some of the bits are good and crisp.

3. Add water to sausage and scrape bits from bottom of pot.

4. Add purée back to pot along with remaining 2 cups broth, beans, and potatoes. Bring to boil and reduce to simmer. Cover and cook 15-20 minutes or until potatoes are tender.

5. Stir in kale and heat through.

6. Season to taste with salt and pepper.

Chicken Tenders

SERVES: 4 | ACTIVE TIME: 10 MINUTES | TOTAL TIME: 25 MINUTES

◑ ¾ cup crushed unsweetened crispy **rice cereal**

◑ ¼ cup gluten-free **seasoned coating mix**

¼ teaspoon **sweet paprika**

1½ pounds **chicken tenders**

1 tablespoon **Soy-Free Vegenaise mayonnaise**

High heat cooking oil for frying

Salt to taste

These super easy chicken tenders satisfy my occasional craving for fried chicken. I use Hodgson Mill Gluten Free Seasoned Coating Mix. Look for it at natural foods stores. The crispy cereal gives the tenders a bit of crunch. If corn is tolerated, crushed corn flakes work just as well.

1. In a medium bowl combine crushed cereal, seasoned coating mix, and paprika.
2. Rinse and pat chicken tenders dry.
3. In a separate bowl toss chicken tenders with mayonnaise to coat.
4. Roll tenders in crumb coating—pressing coating in for better adhesion.
5. Set aside 3-5 minutes.
6. Meanwhile, heat 2 tablespoons oil in a large skillet over medium heat.
7. Fry tenders in batches until both sides are golden brown and chicken is cooked through. Add more oil as needed and turn chicken with care.
8. Finish with a sprinkle of salt.

Stroganoff

4 dried (½ oz) **shiitake mushrooms**

1½ cups hot **water**

1 pound ground beef or **ground bison**

1 teaspoon **salt**, divided

1 tablespoon medium or **high heat cooking oil**

1 medium **onion**, roughly chopped

3 cloves **garlic**, smashed

1½ cups **beef broth**

2 tablespoons superfine **brown rice flour**

2 tablespoons fresh **lemon juice**

1 tablespoon **Worcestershire sauce**

1½ teaspoons **hot sauce**

⅛ teaspoon **black pepper**

⅛ teaspoon dried **dill**

1 cup sliced **crimini mushrooms**, optional

Stroganoff is a comforting dish that can be served over rice or your favorite gluten-free pasta. To dress it up, use a pound of thinly-sliced top sirloin or tenderloin in place of the ground meat. Serve over rice or gluten-free pasta.

1. Soak dried shiitake mushrooms in hot water until soft, about 20 minutes.

2. Meanwhile, in a large skillet brown meat and season with ½ teaspoon salt. Transfer browned meat to a plate.

3. Add oil, onion, and garlic to skillet. Sauté over medium heat until tender.

4. Place mushrooms and soaking water, beef broth, rice flour, lemon juice, Worcestershire sauce, hot sauce, pepper, dill, and remaining ½ teaspoon salt in the container of a high-powered blender. Cover and purée.

5. Add purée back to skillet along with meat and crimini mushrooms.

6. Simmer 5-10 minutes or until mixture thickens.

7. Serve over cooked rice or gluten-free pasta.

Chicken Soup

SERVES: 4-6 | ACTIVE TIME: 15 MINUTES | TOTAL TIME: 30 MINUTES

1 tablespoon **high heat cooking oil**

1 cup peeled and chopped **zucchini**

¼ medium **onion**, chopped

4 cups **water**, divided

4 cups **chicken broth**

¼ cup diced **carrots**

¼ cup diced **celery**

1 teaspoon **granulated onion**

½ teaspoon **salt** or to taste

¼ teaspoon **poultry seasoning**

⅛ teaspoon **white pepper**

¼ teaspoon **hot sauce**

1 **bay leaf**

Pinch **ground turmeric**, optional for color

2 cups uncooked **gluten-free pasta**
or 1 cup uncooked rice

3 cups diced or shredded cooked **chicken**

For the gluten-free among us, a quick run to the store to pick up a can of chicken noodle soup when feeling under the weather is simply a no-go. When someone has the sickies in our house, this is the soup I make. The zucchini adds a bit of creaminess and the turmeric a little color.

1. In large pot, sauté zucchini and onion in oil over medium heat until tender.

2. Transfer zucchini mixture to the container of a blender along with 2 cups water. Cover and purée.

3. Add purée back to pot along with remaining 2 cups water, chicken broth, carrots, celery, granulated onion, salt, poultry seasoning, white pepper, hot sauce, bay leaf, turmeric, and uncooked pasta.

4. Bring to a boil and reduce to a low simmer. Cover and cook just until pasta is al dente or rice is tender—taking care not to overcook.

5. Add chicken and stir to combine. Heat through and salt to taste.

SWEET TREATS

I come from a long line of sweet tooths. Occasionally something triggers the C12H22O11 gene, which I must have inherited, and it drives me to the kitchen to make one of these treats. Thankfully, since cleaning up our diet, the cravings are few and far between. But when they hit, they are real and I give in. After all, what would life be without an occasional dessert!

Strawberry Cheesecake

MAKES: 4-6 INDIVIDUAL SERVINGS | ACTIVE TIME: 30 MINUTES | TOTAL TIME: 3-5 HOURS

1 cup raw **cashews**

¾ cup plain **nondairy yogurt**

⅓ cup **coconut oil** (no substitutions)

¼ cup fresh **lemon juice**

¼ cup **honey**

⅛ teaspoon **salt**

✦ 1 cup allergen-free **graham cracker crumbs** (see page 133)

4 cups hulled and sliced **strawberries**

3 tablespoons melted **honey**

For those who do not tolerate dairy but love their cheesecake, say hello to cashews! Raw cashew nuts are the secret ingredient to many dairy-free, vegan, and raw desserts. For smooth, silky results, a high-powered blender is a must. Omit the crust for a grain-free treat.

1. Soak cashews in a bowl of water for 2-4 hours. Rinse and drain.

2. In the container of a high-powered combine cashews, yogurt, coconut oil, lemon juice, honey, and salt.

3. Cover and purée.

4. Divide graham cracker crumbs evenly among 4-6 small jars or glasses.

5. Divide cheesecake mixture evenly over crumbs. Transfer to refrigerator and chill for 3-4 hours.

6. Meanwhile, in a medium bowl toss strawberries and honey. Refrigerate at least one hour.

7. Top cheesecakes with honey-soaked strawberries and serve.

Banana Bread

MAKES: ONE LOAF | ACTIVE TIME: 15 MINUTES | TOTAL TIME: 1 HOUR 15 MINUTES

1¼ cups mashed ripe **banana**

⅓ cup unsweetened **applesauce**

¼ cup pure **maple syrup**

¼ cup **honey**

¼ cup **palm shortening**

2 tablespoons golden **flaxseed meal**

2 tablespoons **Soy-Free Vegenaise mayonnaise**

1 tablespoon **vanilla extract**

¼ teaspoon **almond extract**, optional

1 cup superfine **brown rice flour**

½ cup **tapioca flour**

⅓ cup **potato starch**

¼ cup **sorghum flour**

1½ teaspoons **baking powder**

½ teaspoon **baking soda**

½ teaspoon **cinnamon**

¼ teaspoon **salt**

This banana bread was inspired by my friend Alisa of GoDairyFree.org. She has a pumpkin bread recipe that is out of this world. With a few modifications it has been transformed into a banana bread that disappears within minutes of being pulled out of the oven. You'll go bananas over this dense and moist quick bread.

1. Preheat oven to 375°F. Grease a standard 9x5-inch glass loaf pan.

2. In a large mixing bowl combine mashed banana, applesauce, maple syrup, honey, shortening, flaxseed meal, mayonnaise, vanilla extract, and almond extract.

3. Using an electric hand mixer beat for 30 seconds.

4. Add remaining ingredients and beat just until combined.

5. Gently scoop batter into prepared loaf pan and smooth top.

6. Bake 10 minutes at 375°F then reduce heat to 325°F and bake an additional 40-45 minutes or until a toothpick inserted in loaf comes out clean.

7. Remove from oven and cool in pan for 5 minutes before turning out onto a wire rack to cool completely.

8. For an extra moist bread, wrap loaf in plastic wrap when still slightly warm.

Macaroons

MAKES: 12-24 | ACTIVE TIME: 30 MINUTES | TOTAL TIME: 2 HOURS 30 MINUTES

⅓ cup **coconut butter**

¼ cup + 2 tablespoons pure **maple syrup**

1 teaspoon **vanilla extract**

⅛ teaspoon **salt**

2 cups unsweetened finely **shredded coconut**

Allergen-free **chocolate chips**, optional

These macaroons are my "safe" go-to treat for holiday gift giving and potlucks. In place of eggs, they are bound with maple syrup and coconut butter and are naturally gluten-free and dairy-free. The result is a crisp on the outside, moist on the inside coconut delight. Coconut butter is a densely nutritious spread made from dried coconut meat (see page 11) and should not be confused with coconut oil.

1. Preheat oven to 325°F. Line a cookie sheet with baking parchment paper.

2. In a large saucepan over low heat melt coconut butter.

3. Whisk in maple syrup, vanilla extract, and salt.

4. Add shredded coconut and stir until combined.

5. Gently pack coconut mixture into a small or medium cookie dough scoop and place on parchment-lined cookie sheet, gently reshaping mounds as needed.

6. Bake 12-15 minutes or until tops begin to turn golden. Take care not to overbake.

7. Remove from oven and transfer cookie sheet to refrigerator and chill for 2 hours. *Do not skip this step.*

8. If desired, drizzle chilled macaroons with chocolate chips that have been melted over low heat. Allow chocolate to harden. Store in an airtight container in refrigerator.

Pumpkin Pie

One half recipe **Pie Dough** (see page 51)

1 can (15 oz) pure **pumpkin**

1 can (14 oz) full-fat **coconut milk**

½ cup pure **maple syrup**

2 tablespoons **tapioca flour**

1 tablespoon **pumpkin pie spice**

1 tablespoon **vanilla extract**

½ teaspoon **salt**

¾ cup **water**

2 teaspoons **agar powder**

Entertaining friends and family on modified diets can be daunting. But working from a short list of ingredients, you can whip up a not-too-sweet no-bake classic that everyone at the feast can enjoy. This pie filling is free of gluten, dairy, eggs, wheat, corn, and soy and is vegan to boot! The pie crust is completely optional. My boys love crustless mini pies made in small ramekins and topped with Whipped Coconut Cream (page 23).

1. Line a 9-inch round pie pan with rolled pie dough (see page 51 for recipe and tips). Transfer to refrigerator or freezer and chill until firm.

2. Preheat oven to 450°F. Prick sides and bottoms of chilled crust with the tines of a fork and bake 10-12 minutes.

3. In the container of a blender combine pumpkin, maple syrup, coconut milk, tapioca flour, pumpkin pie spice, vanilla extract, and salt. Purée; set aside.

4. Add water to a large saucepan, sprinkle the surface with the agar powder. Bring to a boil; reduce to gentle simmer and cook 1-2 minutes. Whisk the pumpkin mixture into the simmering agar. Return to a boil; reduce to gentle simmer and cook 2-3 minutes, stirring occasionally.

5. Pour the hot pie filling into the pre-baked pie shell. Refrigerate until set, about 3-5 hours.

6. Serve chilled or bring to room temperature. Either way, with the help of the agar, the pie will remain firm.

Spritz & Sugar Cookies

MAKES: ABOUT 60 SPRITZ COOKIES | ACTIVE TIME: 15 MINUTES | TOTAL TIME: 1 HOUR 30 MINUTES

1½ tablespoons golden **flaxseed meal**

3 tablespoons cold **water**

✧ 1 tablespoon **vanilla extract**

¾ cup superfine **brown rice flour**

¼ cup **tapioca flour**

¼ cup **potato starch**

✧ 1 teaspoon **baking powder**

✧ ½ cup cold **Earth Balance Soy-Free Buttery Spread**

½ cup granulated cane **sugar**

You can't go wrong with this sugar cookie. Shoot the dough out of a cookie press or roll it into a log, freeze, slice, and bake. These cookies are reminiscent of the Danish Butter Cookies that appear around the holidays and come in those delightful shapes in round metal tins.

1. In a small bowl whisk together flaxseed meal, water, and vanilla extract. Set aside 5 minutes to thicken.

2. In a medium mixing bowl combine flours, potato starch, and baking powder.

3. In a separate medium mixing bowl beat buttery spread and sugar on high for 1 minute using an electric mixer. Add flaxseed mixture and beat on high for 30 seconds. Add flour mixture and beat another 30 seconds.

FOR FREEZE AND SLICE SUGAR COOKIES
Form dough into a ball and roll into a 2-inch diameter log. Wrap in plastic wrap and freeze. When ready to bake; remove plastic wrap and slice into ½-inch disks. Arrange on a baking parchment paper-lined cookie sheet and bake in a pre-heated 375°F oven for 13-15 minutes. Transfer cookies to a wire rack and let cool.

FOR SPRITZ COOKIES
Immediately after mixing dough (do not refrigerate), load cookie press and press out cookies onto <u>unlined</u>, <u>ungreased</u> cookie sheet. Transfer to freezer and freeze 1 hour. Bake in a pre-heated 375°F oven for 10-12 minutes. Transfer cookies to a wire rack and let cool.

Mug Treats

MUG BROWNIE

2 tablespoons **granulated sugar**

2 tablespoons **sweet rice flour**

1½ tablespoons **cocoa powder**

1 tablespoon **coconut flour**

⅛ teaspoon **baking powder**

Pinch **salt**

1 tablespoon chopped **walnuts**, optional

1 tablespoon allergen-free **chocolate chips**

¼ cup + 1 tablespoon **nondairy milk**

1 tablespoon melted **palm shortening**

½ teaspoon **vanilla extract**

MUG CHOCOLATE CHIP COOKIE

¼ cup gluten-free **oat flour**

2 tablespoons **granulated sugar**

Pinch **salt**

Pinch **baking soda**

2 tablespoons **nondairy yogurt**

1 tablespoon unsweetened **applesauce**

1 tablespoon allergen-free **chocolate chips**

½ teaspoon **vanilla extract**

Instant gratification, it's what these recipes deliver. Inspired by one of the many microwave mug cake recipes found online, the Mug Brownie is dense, chocolaty, and fudgy—chocolate bliss delivered in under five minutes! The Mug Chocolate Chip Cookie is a slight adaptation of a recipe found on the blog SiftStirAndSavour.com. A big thank you to Erin for introducing me to cookies in a mug!

1. Grease a small mug.

2. In a small mixing bowl combine ingredients for your mug treat of choice and stir until smooth.

3. Spoon batter into greased mug.

4. Microwave on high for 90 seconds or until top is firm to touch and bounces back when gently pressed. Cooking times will vary by microwave.

5. Allow to cool at least 2-3 minutes. As with traditional brownies and cookies, the longer these treats cool, the firmer they become.

Grind oats into oat flour using a clean coffee grinder, spice grinder, or high-powered blender.

Brownies

MAKES: 16 BROWNIES | ACTIVE TIME: 15 MINUTES | TOTAL TIME: 55 MINUTES

1 cup **granulated sugar**

½ cup **cocoa powder**

2 tablespoons **flaxseed meal**

½ teaspoon **salt**

½ cup unsweetened **applesauce**

1 small (½ cup mashed) ripe **avocado**

¼ cup **palm shortening**

1 tablespoon **vanilla extract**

1¼ cups superfine **brown rice flour**

½ cup **tapioca flour**

¼ cup **rice bran**, optional (see Tips and Tricks)

1 teaspoon **baking powder**

⅓ cup allergen-free **chocolate chips**, optional

These dense, fudgy brownies pack a nutritious secret ingredient that no one will suspect is hidden there—avocado! In baking, the use of avocado allows for a reduction in the amount of fat needed to produce a moist baked good. My boys enjoy these brownies with a cold glass of almond milk (see page 19).

1. Preheat oven to 350°F. Grease an 8x8-inch glass baking dish.

2. In the bowl of a food processor fitted with the "s" blade, combine the sugar, cocoa powder, flaxseed meal, salt, applesauce, avocado, palm shortening, and vanilla extract. Process until super smooth, about 1 minute.

3. Add the flours, rice bran, baking powder, and chocolate chips. Process just until combined.

4. Spoon batter into prepared baking dish. Spread using a rubber spatula and smooth top with moistened fingertips.

5. Bake 40-45 minutes.

6. Allow to cool completely before cutting. Store in an airtight container in refrigerator.

» Tips and Tricks «

☞ *Prefer brownies on the cakier side? Be sure to add the ¼ cup rice bran.*

☞ *Use Dutch process cocoa powder for extra dark brownies.*

Lower Sugar Option

Reduce sugar or maple syrup to ¼ cup and sweeten to taste with plain or vanilla liquid stevia concentrate.

Pudding

FOR VANILLA PUDDING

½ cup cold **water**

1¾ tablespoons **gelatin**

1 ounce **cocoa butter**

¼ cup granulated cane **sugar**

¼ cup pure **maple syrup**

2 (14 oz) cans full-fat **coconut milk**

✪ 1 tablespoon **vanilla extract**

1 teaspoon **vanilla powder**

Pinch **salt**

Dash **ground turmeric** for color, optional

FOR CHOCOLATE PUDDING

½ cup cold **water**

1½ tablespoons **gelatin**

3 ounces allergen-free **dark chocolate**

¼ cup **granulated sugar**

¼ cup **pure maple syrup**

2 (14 oz) cans full-fat **coconut milk**

✪ 1 teaspoon **vanilla extract**

Pinch **salt**

I find these puddings reminiscent of Snack Pack pudding. Cocoa butter adds a remarkable white chocolate creaminess to the Vanilla Pudding while dark chocolate lends richness to the Chocolate Pudding. A good whipping with a hand mixer just prior to serving gives these sweet treats a super silky mouthfeel. Use these puddings in place of the boxed variety in pies and parfaits.

---

1. Add water to a small saucepan and sprinkle gelatin over surface. Warm mixture over low heat just until gelatin dissolves.

2. In a double boiler melt cocoa butter (or dark chocolate for Chocolate Pudding). Whisk in sugar and maple syrup and cook over medium heat until sugar begins to dissolve.

3. Whisk in coconut milk, dissolved gelatin, and remaining ingredients. Continue to cook until steam rises from surface.

4. Pour pudding into a medium mixing bowl or individual serving cups, and cover with plastic wrap. Chill until set, about 4-5 hours. For an extra silky pudding, chill in medium mixing bowl and beat until super smooth using an electric mixer prior to serving.

⟫ Tips *and* Tricks ⟪

☞ *A large, rounded bottom stainless steel bowl atop a large saucepan filled ¼ full with water makes a great stand-in for a double boiler.*

☞ *Leftover pudding may be beat and poured into popsicle molds for a frosty pudding pop.*

Tasty Variation

Add 2-4 tablespoons
Dutch process cocoa
powder for a decadent
chocolate ice cream.

Vanilla Ice Cream

MAKES: ABOUT 1½ QUARTS | ACTIVE TIME: 5 MINUTES | TOTAL TIME: 30 MINUTES

1 (14 oz) can full-fat **coconut milk**

1⅓ cups cold **nondairy milk** of choice

½ cup **honey** or granulated sugar

¾ teaspoon **vanilla powder**

½ heaping teaspoon **guar gum**, optional

Pinch **salt**

One of my most treasured cookbooks is *The Spunky Coconut Dairy-Free Ice Cream* by Kelly Brozyna. I agree with Kelly that guar gum—a natural food thickener derived from the guar plant—is the secret to smooth and creamy nondairy ice cream. This recipe makes a great base from which to experiment and create your favorite ice cream flavor.

1. Add all ingredients to the container of a blender. Cover and blend.

2. Pour mixture into a 1½ quart ice cream machine and follow the manufacturer's instructions.

3. Most ice cream machines produce a soft serve consistency. For a hard scoop, spread ice cream in a shallow dish and freeze until firm.

Tips and Tricks

☞ *Add a "French vanilla" creamy tint with a pinch of ground turmeric.*

☞ *For Mint Chocolate Chip blend in a few fresh spinach leaves and then add in a small handful of allergen-free chocolate chips and peppermint extract to taste. For Rich Dark Chocolate blend in 2-4 tablespoons Dutch process cocoa powder.*

☞ *1 tablespoon vanilla extract may be used in place of vanilla powder.*

Vanilla Cupcakes

MAKES: 12 CUPCAKES | ACTIVE TIME: 15 | TOTAL TIME: 35 MINUTES

FOR THE VANILLA CUPCAKES

2 tablespoons golden **flaxseed meal**

1 tablespoon whole **psyllium husk**

½ cup **nondairy milk**

✤ 1 tablespoon **vanilla extract**

2 teaspoons fresh **lemon juice**

¾ cup **granulated cane sugar**

⅓ cup **palm shortening**

1 cup + 2 tablespoons **Bob's Red Mill AP GF Flour**

¼ cup **tapioca flour**

1 teaspoon **vanilla powder**

✤ ¾ teaspoon **baking powder**

¼ teaspoon **baking soda**

¼ teaspoon **salt**

½ cup boiling **water**

FOR THE VERY VANILLA ICING

✤ 2 tablespoons **Earth Balance Soy-Free Buttery Spread**

2 tablespoons **palm shortening**

1⅔ cups **powdered cane sugar**

1½ teaspoons **vanilla powder**

Pinch **salt**

2 tablespoons **nondairy milk**

These heavier on the sweet cupcakes are what I make for birthdays and special occasions. Glaze them, top them with Chocolate Ganache (see page 135), or pipe on Very Vanilla Frosting.

FOR THE VANILLA CUPCAKES

1. Preheat oven to 350°F. Line 12 muffin cups with paper liners.

2. In a large mixing bowl whisk together flaxseed meal, psyllium husk, milk, vanilla extract, and lemon juice. Set aside 3-4 minutes to thicken.

3. Add sugar and palm shortening to thickened flaxseed mixture and beat on high for 30 seconds using an electric mixer.

4. Add flours, vanilla powder, baking powder, baking soda, and salt and beat to combine.

5. Add boiling water and beat at low-medium speed for one minute.

6. Divide batter evenly among muffin cups, about ½ full. Bake 19-21 minutes or until a toothpick inserted into cupcakes comes out clean.

FOR THE VERY VANILLA FROSTING

1. In a medium bowl beat buttery spread and palm shortening until smooth using an electric mixer.

2. Add powdered sugar, vanilla powder, and salt. Beat to combine.

3. Add milk and beat until smooth.

4. Tint with natural food coloring or add seeds of one vanilla bean if desired.

5. Frost cupcakes once completely cooled.

Graham Crackers

MAKES: VARIES | ACTIVE TIME:15 MINUTES | TOTAL TIME: 1 HOUR 10 MINUTES

¼ cup brown sugar or **coconut sugar**

¼ cup golden **flaxseed meal**

¼ cup + 2 tablespoons **palm shortening**

¼ cup **honey**

3 tablespoons **water**

✛ ½ teaspoon **vanilla extract**

1 cup superfine **brown rice flour**

¼ cup **teff flour**

¼ cup **potato starch**

¼ cup **tapioca flour**

✛ ½ teaspoon **baking powder**

¼ heaping teaspoon **baking soda**

¼ teaspoon ground **cinnamon**

½ teaspoon **salt**

As I wrapped up the writing of this book, I realized there was one American Classic I had left out: Graham Crackers! Without them there would be no s'mores or graham cracker crusts. Now that just wouldn't do, would it?

1. In the bowl of a food processor fitted with the "s" blade combine sugar, flaxseed meal, palm shortening, honey, water, and vanilla extract. Process for 30 seconds.

2. Add remaining ingredients and process until a soft dough forms.

3. Form dough into a ball and place between two sheets of baking parchment paper. Roll to ⅛-inch thick.

4. Leaving sheets of parchment paper intact, carefully transfer to a cookie sheet and place in freezer to chill 30 minutes.

5. Preheat oven to 325°F.

6. Remove rolled dough from freezer and peel away top layer of parchment. Using a pizza cutter or sharp knife, cut crackers to desired size. Prick tops with the tines of a fork or a bamboo skewer.

7. Bake 16-18 minutes. Slide sheet of crackers onto a cooling rack. Let cool completely. Crackers will crisp up as they cool. If some of the crackers need a bit more crisping, simply return to a warm, powered-off oven for 10-15 minutes.

Chocolate Cheesecake

MAKES: ONE 8-INCH ROUND CAKE | ACTIVE TIME: 30 MINUTES | TOTAL TIME: 7 HOURS

FOR THE CRUST

1¾ cups **raw walnuts**

¼ cup **flaxseed meal**

2 tablespoons **cocoa powder**

✦ ¼ teaspoon **baking powder**

Pinch of **salt**

¼ cup melted **coconut oil** (no substitutions)

2 tablespoons **maple syrup**

FOR THE FILLING

1 cup **raw cashew** pieces

⅓ cup **granulated sugar**

¼ cup **cocoa powder**

¼ scant teaspoon **salt**

⅔ cup plain or vanilla **nondairy yogurt**

⅓ cup melted **coconut oil** (no substitutions)

1 tablespoon fresh **lime juice**

✦ 1 teaspoon **vanilla extract**

FOR THE GANACHE

⅓ cup **coconut cream** (see page 23)

⅓ cup allergen-free **chocolate chips**

Looking for a winning recipe that will surely impress the boss? Give this one a go. For smooth, silky results, a high-powered blender is a must. Enjoy this cheesecake with or without a crust. For the mini versions pictured, use a mini cheesecake pan.

1. Soak cashews in a bowl of water for 2-4 hours.

2. Preheat oven to 350°F. Line the bottom of a 6- or 8-inch round springform pan with baking parchment paper.

3. Add crust ingredients to the bowl of a food processor fitted with the "s" blade. Pulse to graham cracker crust texture. Firmly press crust into pan. Bake 10 minutes and let cool completely.

4. Rinse and drain cashews. Add to the container of a high-powered blender along with remaining filling ingredients. Cover; blend on high until smooth.

5. Pour cheesecake filling over cooled crust. Tap pan repeatedly on counter to release trapped air bubbles. Freeze 3-5 hours or until firm.

6. Make Chocolate Ganache by warming coconut cream over medium heat in a small saucepan. Remove from heat and stir in chocolate chips. Continue stirring until smooth.

7. Remove cheesecake from freezer 15 minutes prior to serving. Remove from pan and set on a decorative plate. Top with slightly warm, but not hot, ganache and serve.

8. Keep any leftovers in freezer for a firmer texture or in refrigerator for a creamier texture.

Marshmallows

MAKES: 64 1-INCH MARSHMALLOWS | ACTIVE TIME: 30 MINUTES | TOTAL TIME: 4 HOURS 30 MINUTES

CANE SUGAR MARSHMALLOWS

Potato starch for dusting

1 cup cold **water**, divided

⊕ 2 teaspoons **vanilla extract**

¼ teaspoon **salt**

2½ tablespoons unflavored powdered **gelatin**

1 cup **granulated cane sugar**

HONEY OR MAPLE SYRUP MARSHMALLOWS

Potato starch for dusting

½ cup cold **water**

⊕ 2 teaspoons **vanilla extract**

¼ teaspoon **salt**

2½ tablespoons unflavored powdered **gelatin**

1 cup **honey** or pure maple syrup

Yes you can. You can make marshmallows! These pillowy bombs of sweetness pair deliciously with a chunk of dark chocolate and a crisp graham cracker (page 133).

1. Lightly coat an 8x8-inch square baking dish with oil. Generously dust sides and bottom with potato starch.

2. *For Cane Sugar Marshmallows:* Add ½ cup water, vanilla extract, and salt to a deep mixing bowl or bowl of a stand mixer. Sprinkle gelatin over surface of liquid and set aside. In a medium saucepan combine ½ cup water and sugar and proceed to Step 4.

3. *For Honey or Maple Syrup Marshmallows:* Add ½ cup water, vanilla extract, and salt to a deep mixing bowl or bowl of a stand mixer. Sprinkle gelatin over surface of liquid and set aside. Into a medium saucepan pour the honey **or** maple syrup and proceed to Step 4.

4. Bring contents of saucepan to a boil over medium-high heat. Continue to boil until a digital thermometer registers the boiling liquid at 235°F—the low end of the soft ball candy stage.

5. Immediately remove from heat.

6. Working quickly and carefully, beat hot liquid into gelatin mixture using an electric mixer. Beat until mixture thickens, turns white, and gently falls in ribbons when the beaters are lifted from bowl, about 4-6 minutes.

7. Pour mixture into prepared pan. Let set 3-4 hours at room temperature.

8. Run a knife around edge of pan and unmold onto a starch-dusted surface. Slice into 1-inch cubes using a sharp, starch-dusted knife. Dust marshmallows with more starch to prevent sticking.

9. Store in an airtight container at room temp for up to one week or freeze.

Top It Off

This cake pairs well with
fresh berries and
Whipped Coconut Cream
(see page 23).

Flourless Chocolate Cake

SERVES: 6-8 | ACTIVE TIME: 10 MINUTES | TOTAL TIME: 5-7 HOURS

½ cup raw **cashews**

4 tablespoons Dutch process **cocoa powder**, divided

2 tablespoons **coconut oil** (no substitutions)

½ cup allergen-free **chocolate chips**

½ cup plain, unsalted cooked **black beans**

2 tablespoons **coconut flour**

½ cup lukewarm **water**

3 tablespoons granulated sugar or melted **honey**

🌐 ¾ teaspoon **baking powder**

Flourless Chocolate Cake, Chocolate Torte, Chocolate Decadence—the three are closely related. Traditionally these dense, fudgy cakes call for hefty measures of cocoa, eggs, sugar, butter, and cream. It's no wonder this sweet also goes by the name Death by Chocolate. Be forewarned, a little slice goes a long way.

---

1. Soak cashews in a bowl of water for 2-4 hours.

2. Preheat oven to 325°F. Oil bottom and sides of a 5- or 6-inch round spring-form pan. Dust with 1 tablespoon cocoa powder.

3. In a small saucepan melt coconut oil and chocolate chips over very low heat, stirring constantly.

4. Rinse and drain cashews and black beans and add to the container of a high-powered blender along with warm chocolate mixture, remaining 3 tablespoons cocoa powder, coconut flour, water, and honey (**do not** add baking powder at this time). Cover and blend on high until super smooth.

5. Add baking powder. Cover and blend on low 5-10 seconds or just until incorporated.

6. Pour into prepared pan and bake 40-45 minutes.

7. Remove cake from oven and chill 4-6 hours to set. Run knife around edge of cake and remove from pan. Serve chilled.

» Tips and Tricks «

☞ *No time to soak the cashews? Soften in hot water for 10 minutes.*

☞ *Cake will rise during baking and fall during cooling.*

INDEX